SMASHMOUTH

Attitude Between the Lines

by Roland Lazenby

ADDAX
PUBLISHING
GROUP

Published by Addax Publishing Group
Copyright © 1997 by Roland Lazenby
Edited by Susan Storey
Designed by Randy Breeden
Cover Design by Jerry Hirt
Cover Photos by: Vernon Biever, Scott Cunningham and Tim Umphrey

For information address:
Addax Publishing Group
8643 Hauser Drive, Suite 235, Lenexa, Kansas 66215

ISBN: 1-886110-26-3

Distributed to the trade by Andrews McMeel
4520 Main Street, Kansas City, Missouri 64111-7701

Printed in the United States of America

Library of Congress Cataloging - in - Publication Data

Lazenby, Roland
    Smashmouth : attitude between the lines / by Roland Lazenby.
        p.   cm.
    ISBN 1-886110-26-3
    1. National Football League. @. Football—United States.
3. Football players—United States.   I. Title.
GV955.5.N35L39 1997
796.332'0973—dc21   97-35121
                                                                        CIP

Author's Acknowledgments

I want to thank the following people for granting the interviews necessary for this book. Some were conducted at the Footaction Quarterback Challenge in Orlando, Florida. Others were done at the Official All-Star Cafe in Myrtle Beach, South Carolina. Still others were conducted around games and practices. Those interviewed included Jerome Bettis, Bob Dozier, Kordell Stewart, Warren Moon, Sammy Baugh, Keyshawn Johnson, Gus Frerotte, Heath Shuler, Chester McGlockton, Eric Dickerson, Kerry Collins, Steve Young, Red Batty, Eugene Chung, Edgar Bennett, Reggie White, Darren Sharper, Gladys Bettis, Leo Goeas, Emmitt Smith, Nate Newton, Drew Bledsoe, Dan Marino, Boomer Esaison, Rick Mirer and Tim Brown.

I would also like to thank the public relations staffs of the Dallas Cowboys, Green Bay Packers, San Francisco 49ers, and St. Louis Rams.

Also providing much help were Mike Shank of the Official All-Star Cafe and Laurie Goldberg of Pinnacle trading cards. Larry Canale of Tuff Stuff Publications was another champ, as was David Levin, who helped provide research for the project.

The work of numerous writers, including Howard Balzer, Charles Pierce, Peter Richmond, Joe Gergen, Don Pasquarelli, Mickey Spagnola, Gordon Forbes, Austin Murphy, Paul Zimmerman, Scott Ostler, Richard Justice, Mike Wilbon, Rick Weinberg and many others provided valuable background.

I also made use of a variety of publications including Team NFL, Sports Illustrated, Sport, The Sporting News, USA Today, GQ, Esquire, Lindy's Pro Football Annual, Street & Smith's Pro Football Annual, the Sacramento Bee, the LA Times, the New York Times, the New York Post, Athalon Sports Annuals, the Charlotte Observer, the San Jose Mercury News, the San Francisco Chronicle, the San Francisco Examiner, the Raleigh News and Observer, the Dallas Morning News, the Houston Post, Pro Football Weekly, the Boston Globe, the Boston Herald, the Washington Post, the Baltimore Sun, and the Washington Times.

I am also deeply indebted to Bob Snodgrass, publisher of Addax Publishing Group, and his many fine assistants, including Darcie Kidson, Susan Storey, Brad Breon, Michelle Washington and designer Randy Breeden.

Beyond them, I owe the greatest debt to my family, sweet Karen, Jenna, Henry and Morgan, an A team if there ever was one.

Roland Lazenby
1997

It's blitz, hitz and no quitz in today's NFL.

CONTENTS

Intro/SMASHMOUTH!!!

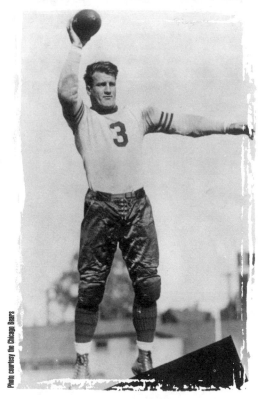

Bronko Nagurski was a block of knock in pro football's early years.

Apologies to the brotha Snoop Doggy Dogg, but football is da reeaal shiznit, uknowhatI'msayin'? Fans been havin' much love for the game for a long time, since the dayz when Jim Thorpe laced metal rivets into his shoulder pads for the first edition of pop 'n' drop and even later when Jack Tatum did his chillin' by killin'.

Smashmoufootball!!! It's da LEAGUE, da iNeffYELL, da land of hard hits and cold killaz, where atmospheric violence can make muthaphreakin' Compton look like a love in. Yo, baby, it's da House of Pain, a drain on the brain wit' no gain, uknowhatI'msayin'? Like the sign says, better snap yo' strap before entering.

So what up with the new bad boyz in the league? Who's dopest? Brett Favre or Drew Bledsoe? Kordell Stewart or Gus Frerotte? Mark Brunell or Kerry Collins? Curtis Martin or Terrell Davis?

Is Keyshawn fly? Or is the brotha just another rookie making noyz? Who's sellin' out? Who's got attitude? Who's got gratitude for the latitude?

You got questions? They got nuttin' but answers in the land of Smashmouf. Da real shiznit!!! Where all the homeys got headgear, where the only speed posted is balls-out smokin', and it's blitz, hitz and no quits, where each and every day you're flirtin' with hurtin', uknowhatI'msayin'?

Smashmouf!!! Da one 'n' only sho' 'nuff shiznit!!!

When Red Grange was tearing up the National Football League as a rookie in 1925, he was invited to the White House to visit President Calvin Coolidge. "This is Red Grange, who plays with the Bears," said a senator who introduced the Galloping Ghost to the President.

"Coolidge shook my hand," Grange later recalled, "and said, 'Nice to meet you, young man. I've always liked animal acts.'"

Coolidge, of course, was revealing that he knew absolutely nothing about pro football (back in the 1920s, not very many people did). Yet, in a sense, Coolidge had managed to sum up the very essence of the sport.

"This is a game for madmen," Vince Lombardi, the great Green Bay Packers coach, once observed.

There's little reason to wonder then why from its earliest beginnings the NFL has been populated by strange beasts, hard-drinking, hard-driving men who possessed unhealthy levels of testosterone.

Men who smiled toothlessly at the idea of smashmouth football.

Men like rebel running back Joe Don Looney, who used to make a show of eating light bulbs and jumping out of third-floor windows, who played for a variety of teams, most of which refused to keep him for more than a few weeks because he was so crazy. He used to like to sleep in cemeteries "because it's so peaceful there." Detroit coach Harry Gilmer once asked Looney to carry a play into the game for the quarterback. "You need a messenger," Looney said, "call Western Union."

Men like Johnny "Blood" McNally, who was once asked for an autograph by a young lady and responded by slashing his wrist and signing in blood. The resulting wound took numerous stitches to close, according to Grange, who witnessed the whole thing.

Like San Francisco 49ers tackle Bob St. Clair, who was fond of eating raw meat, including liver. In restaurants, he would ask for his steaks right out of the icebox, then eat the bloody meat with a smile.

Men like the Chicago Bears' late, great fullback, Bronko Nagurski. "I remember one game," Bears coach George Halas once recalled, "his head was down, charging like a bull, Nagurski blasted through two tacklers at the goal line as if they were a pair of old-time saloon doors, through the end zone, and full speed into the brick retaining wall behind it. The sickening thud reverberated throughout the stadium."

Staggering, Nagurski came over to the bench and told Halas, "That last guy really gave me a good lick."

Another time Nagurski was horsing around with some friends on the second floor of a hotel room when he crashed through a window and fell into the busy street below.

"What happened?" asked a police officer who rushed up to check on the commotion.

"I don't know," Nagurski replied as he got groggily to his feet. "I just got here myself."

Men like Bobby Layne, the legendary partier and signal-caller supreme. Tackle Alex Karras recalled riding with Layne one booze-filled night during training camp: "I looked up and saw that he had his right foot up on the dashboard, the left one stuck out the window. And while he was singing, I noticed that the accelerator had jammed. I checked the speedometer. The needle shivered at 100 miles per hour, and we're roaring down the expressway with things shaking and bouncing inside the car. All the while, Layne's singing 'Ida Red, Ida Red' (his favorite song). So I finally got down off the seat, and on my knees I begged him to stop the car. But we kept moving down that expressway with his feet still in the same position and a look of contentment all over his face."

Men like John Riggins. A major maniac, he held out from the Jets in 1973. When he finally signed a contract, he showed up shirtless with leather pants and a Mohawk haircut. "Damndest sight you ever saw," said Jets coach Weeb Ewbank. "He had that Mohawk haircut and he was stripped to the waist and he was wearing leather pants and a derby hat with a feather in it. It must have been what the sale of Manhattan Island looked like."

Men like Kansas City Chiefs center Jack Rudnay, who once cut the crotch out of his football pants to teach rookie quarterback David Jaynes a lesson. "Everything's hanging out," recalled teammate Tom Keating. "Rudnay's over the ball. Jaynes looks left, looks right, just like he's been taught. He calls his signals. . . 'Brown right, X left, ready, set. . .' and he reaches down for the ball . . . whooo! The ball goes flying."

Like Dick Butkus. The Bears' great 'backer was one of the game's dirtiest players. "I never intentionally try to hurt another player," he once confessed, "unless it's during something real important, like a league game."

Like Ted Hendricks, who played for Baltimore, Green Bay and Oakland. Also known as "Kick-'Em-In-The-Head" Ted and the "Mad Stork," he showed up for his first Raiders practice in full uniform, wearing a spiked German army helmet, riding a horse, with a traffic cone for a lance and declaring, "I'm ready to play."

Like John Matuszak, another well-traveled problem child who wound up with the Raiders. Matuszak was once cut by the Washington Redskins. Asked why, coach George Allen replied, "Vodka and Valium, the breakfast of champions." Matuszak was known to live in the trunk of his car on occasion. Posed nude for Playgirl magazine. Hobbies included dismantling bars and accosting strange women and hoisting them onto his shoulder.

Like Tim Rossovich, longtime Eagles linebacker/noseguard who perpetrated many zany acts over his career, including setting his own hair on fire, swallowing lighted cigarettes, chewing glass, jumping out of sorority house windows. Once he crammed a swallow into his mouth, walked into a team meeting and opened wide, leaving teammates and coaches flabbergasted when the bird flew out. Once, wearing only shaving cream over his entire body, he enjoyed a run through a major Los Angeles intersection.

Like Gene "Big Daddy" Lipscomb, the great Baltimore Colts tackle, a hard partier who died of a heroin overdose. He was supposedly the first player to celebrate a quarterback sack. One of his teammates used to sell cemetery plots and bugged everyone in the Colts' locker room to buy a plot. Finally, Big Daddy gave in. "I'll take two in the shade," he said.

Like Jack Tatum. Nicknamed "The Assassin" by the Raiders' publicity office, Tatum was known for his shattering hits and headhunting tackles. He devised a scoring system with fellow Raider DB George Atkinson where they got one point if a receiver limped off the field, two if he had to be helped. Atkinson himself was once labelled a "criminal" by Pittsburgh coach Chuck Noll for a stunning forearm he delivered to the head of Steeler receiver Lynn Swann. Many think Atkinson was perhaps the meanest man in the history of this very mean game. "I treat receivers the way I would treat a burglar in my house," he said. "Don't nobody mess with my things."

Like Skip Thomas, another Raiders defensive back. He was nicknamed "Dr. Death" and was so proud of it that he had it painted on the sides of his white Corvette, in gold-leaf, foot-high letters. He spent his years in the Raiders' defensive backfield making sure he lived up to that name.

It is this mindset of smashmouth that today's highly paid, college-educated football stars are faced with inheriting. Asked to define "smashmouth" football, a longtime coach offered that it was "the strategy of overcoming an opponent through the use of acts of controlled violence."

But it's actually more than that. It's a certain strain of insanity, a bug-eyed intensity that has infected footballers since the sport's earliest days. They just love that special kind of up-close and personal contact, breath in your face, spit in your eye. It's a desire to put the other guy's teeth in the dirt, preferably separated from his gums.

There have been literally hundreds of reprobates, mad dogs and lunatics drawn to the violence of Sunday mayhem. The sport began more than a century ago as a seedy business that grew out of the dreams and aspirations of a collection of rogue promoters, tramp athletes and sociopaths. Never did they fathom that today's players would become millionaires for their dirt-kickin', snot-slingin', eye-gougin', ball-bustin', bone-rattlin' antics.

All of which raises this most essential question: Are the members of today's Attitude Generation able to live up to the indecency of their legacy, or has all the money made them little more than a bunch of wimp-ass show dogs, preenin' and prancin' for the cameras, who sneak away between plays to dial their stockbrokers on cell phones? Are they real football players, or just a bunch of high-priced phonies?

Certainly Bryan Cox has the loony part down. After the grand-standing defender moved from the Miami Dolphins to the Bears, he wore only his jockstrap and cleats while running time trials near the windows of the team's offices. "Gave the secretaries a thrill," quipped Chicago quarterback Erik Kramer.

Is this generation all about cheap thrillz, or is it made up of honest-to-God lunatics worthy of football's great heritage? Is it about high-priced punks like Troy Aikman, who sneer when a 10-year-old kid asks for an autograph? Or is it about high ballers like Brett Favre, ready to make eye contact with the world?

Read on as we journey through the NFL of the 1990s, trying to separate the real shiznit from the imposters and frauds posing as stars and cashing big checks they don't earn.

The reeaal shiznit!!! When you find it, it'll shine.

Part I
The Quarterback Challenge

*"You gotta be a football hero
to get along with the beautiful girls..."*
— an old song

Sonny Jurgenson, who labored 18 seasons in the NFL, once remarked that playing pro quarterback **"is like holding group therapy for 50,000 people a week."**

The position is among the most visible, the most demanding in all of sport. And, as Jurgenson or any Hall of Famer will tell you, no other role draws more emotional response from the fans. Over the course of a game, quarterbacks and their publics run the extremes of love and hate, admiration and spite. There is seldom a middle ground.

"Pro football gave me a good perspective to enter politics," former Bills QB Jack Kemp once quipped. "I'd already been booed, cheered, cut, sold, traded and hung in effigy."

It should be pointed out that Jurgy and Kemp both played in the days before megamillion dollar contracts. The fans they faced were actually mild compared to the testiness you find in modern stadiums, where ticket prices are outrageous and beers cost four bucks.

Nor did the old-timers have to contend with learning high-tech offenses, reading complex, multiple defenses, and listening to a haranguing coach over the helmet radio headset.

All of which means that playing quarterback today is more challenging than ever.

Nevertheless, the basic job still requires that same old tricky mix of talents. Leadership and the passing gun rate high. But so do fearlessness, competitive spirit, physical toughness, presence of mind, mobility, excellent vision, luck, determination and a knack for winning. Add to that a level of self-confidence that routinely borders on arrogance and you have a recipe that few athletes can fill.

Which is just the reason why the entire sport—from general managers to fans—maintains a fascination for young quarterbacks. The question is always there, hanging in the air with the barked signals and the singular smell of pads and sweat: Is he the one?

More often than not, the answer is a resounding no.

The corridors of the NFL's stadiums are littered with the lost hopes placed in the likes of Cliff Stoudt, Mark Malone, Browning Nagle, Timm Rosenbach, Todd Marinovich and a host of others.

The league has waged huge sums that one or more of them would emerge to stardom.

Throughout the early 1990s, this QB star search reached new levels of intensity, as the established old guns—Joe Montana, Randall Cunningham, Steve Young, John Elway, Dan Marino, Jim Kelly and Warren Moon—creaked closer to retirement.

Of the league's next generation of stars, the Cowboys' Troy Aikman has the obvious edge with his having led Dallas to a fistful of Super Bowl championships. Next on the list of would-be heroes is Green Bay's Brett Favre, followed by New England's Drew Bledsoe.

Dan the Man set standards for the league's rising star QBs.

From there, it's a group of young guys eager to prove they can lead their teams to championships. Jacksonville's Mark Brunell, Carolina's Kerry Collins, Cincinnati's Jeff Blake, Chicago's Rick Mirer, Pittsburgh's Kordell Stewart, New Orleans' Heath Shuler and Washington's Gus Frerotte all have big-time aspirations.

Each of them has shown the combination of skills and luck to get them a shot at a starting job in the NFL. But the only way to keep it is to win. That, said the late, legendary Paul Brown, is the real test of a signal caller: Did his team win?

To talk about these and other issues, I visited with quarterbacks young and old. What follows, in this first part of "Smashmouth!!!", are their stories, how they became, or want to become, football heroes.

Chapter 1/First And Last

Heath Shuler was looking to find a home in New Orleans after losing out in Washington.

t has been nothing but painful, this business of Heath Shuler and Gus Frerotte trading places. Surprising as it was, one's fall and the other's rise shouldn't have been unexpected. After all, if you play quarterback in the National Football League, it seems fairly obvious from the gitgo that people are looking to plant a hurtin' on you. All told, there are probably a million different ways to get sacked, and Heath Shuler has already discovered about 200,000 of 'em in his young career.

I'm making these astute observations here at the Quarterback Challenge at Disneyworld in Orlando, Florida, where all the quarterbacks and would-be quarterbacks in the NFL gather in the springtime to have their pictures taken for trading cards and marketing efforts and other silliness. The weekend of media sessions is anchored by the Quarterback Challenge, an offseason event that tests the athleticism of quarterbacks in a competition of running and throwing skills.

Right now, though, the competition is between Shuler's georgeous girlfriend and the plates of steaks, ribs, shrimp, crab legs and other delicacies offered up at the banquet sponsored for the quarterbacks and sleazy media types like me. Either I sit here chatting with Heath's girlfriend, who has a face and eyes you can just get lost in, or I get up for another plate of shrimp and crab legs and yet another glass of frothy beverage.

In a moment of weakness, I elect to forego the food to spend more time with Heath's honey. She, too, has thoughts on her mind other than food. In fact, she wants to dance. Once, she tells me, she was at a Bob Evans restaurant with Heath and his brother Benjie, who is a receiver at the University of Tennessee, where Heath himself was a star quarterback and where Heath's girlfriend is currently a senior. Anyway, the three of them were at this Bob

Evans restaurant when she and Heath's brother Benjie got up to dance, right there in front of everybody; they just felt like it, she said, which is what most young people say when they want to jump up and kick a little shit.

She, like the Shulers, is from the Carolina mountains that run along the Tennessee border, not far from Cherokee County, North Carolina, where Heath grew up to become a star quarterback. Like I said, she has a face you could just get lost in. She's a broadcast major, but she's not sure she wants to be a TV personality because she knows that to work in the business you have to want to kill. Killing people doesn't seem to be on her list of priorities.

She does want to dance, though. The band is serving up all the Macarena you can stand.

But poor Heath is just not up to it, never mind that he's at another of those heavenly excess parties, the kind that his homeboys back in Cherokee County would rave about for weeks, with mounds of jumbo shrimp and crab claws beckoning from tubs of ice, slabs of barbecued beef ribs and trays of rib eyes soaking in their own juice, and all the bourbon and beer you can drink. But Heath's not gonna eat much and he's not gonna drink at all. And he's definitely not gonna dance.

You see, right at the moment, Shuler doesn't think he's done anything to deserve all of this. Heck, somebody even offered him a chance to make a pile of money endorsing a product recently. But he turned it down. An athlete turning down product-endorsement money? That's sorta like water refusing to run down hill.

Hearing that would normally make you worry about what they're teaching kids in those classes at UT over in Knoxville. But it's just his mountain ethic at work. You can see from his swarthy good looks that he's probably got some of that strong Cherokee character running in his blood. Plus he's pure hillbilly, a shining product of Appalachian mountain culture, from his twang to his easy grin.

About the only thing that could blunt this good countenance was the cross-talkin', two-timin' ways of the Washington Redskins. And that's just what happened to nice, young Heath Shuler. What he thought was a dream turned out to be nothing but nightmare.

It wasn't supposed to be that way, of course.

The Washington Redskins selected Shuler with the third overall pick of the 1994 draft and signed him to an eight-year, $19.25 million contract. They figured that in two years their young hotshot quarterback would begin his emergence.

Almost as an afterthought, they took Gus Frerotte way down in the seventh round (the 197th player taken overall). The Redskins really had no plans to take a second rookie quarterback, but Frerotte, from the University of Tulsa, had an arm and skills that were just too good to pass up.

It's funny how things work out sometimes. To give his agent leverage, Shuler held out of camp that fall of 1994 to force the team to pack extra dollars into his contract. He arrived 13 days late and light-years behind in his preparation for the season.

Frerotte, on the other hand, signed for minimal money (less than $500,000 over three years) and was ready for camp bright and early. It also helped that he had played in a pro-style offense at Tulsa and was ready for the transition to the NFL.

To try to help their young quarterbacks adjust, the Washington staff had attempted to simplify their offense during the 1994 season. But the team, too, was searching for answers with a new coaching staff headed by Norv Turner, which only compounded Shuler's late start. So things weren't as stable as the coaches and players would have liked. As a starter that fall of 1994, Shuler threw three TDs and eight interceptions.

"Everything just ran together the first year," Shuler would later explain. "We were changing plays from week to week. I'd think I had the offense down pat one week, then the game plan would come in for the next game, and it would be like we were running a different offense."

The coaches began complaining that Shuler had trouble making decisions on the field in the heat of battle, which is exactly the problem with most rookie quarterbacks. Tom Landry, the great Cowboys coach, once explained that the germination period of an NFL quarterback is about five seasons. It usually takes that long for a young guy to learn the ropes.

It's this mental aspect of the game that makes the challenge so difficult for rookies, says new San Diego head coach Kevin Gilbride.

"The quarterback is subjected to much more scrutiny than anyone else," he explained. "The mental aspect is greater. You have to know what you're doing, what the defense is doing and then correct your teammates, too. They have to do what you tell them to do. Until a quarterback has command of what he's doing, he can't be what everyone expects him to be—leader of the franchise."

It didn't help that the rest of the Redskins' roster was in transition that season, with constant changes on both the offensive and defensive lines. As a result, the once-proud Redskins struggled to get a win.

Then Shuler got injured, and Frerotte came in as a backup and won his first game against the Indianapolis Colts. It was the seventh week of the season, and Gus gunned the ball for 226 yards and two touchdowns, enough to earn him NFC Player of the Week honors. Instantly he was a fan favorite. His teammates loved his gutsiness, too.

Shuler, meanwhile, was still the front-runner, but he spent much of his first two seasons in Washington battling injuries and inconsistent play. And again Frerotte stepped in as his replacement in 1995, and threw for better than 2,700 yards, another set of impressive results.

The Redskins' brass still looked at trading Frerotte over the summer of 1996. The St. Louis Rams were the primary suitors. The planned trade called for the Rams to send Sean Gilbert to Washington for Frerotte. But the Rams got cold feet and decided to take the Redskins' sixth overall pick in the draft (which they used to select running back Lawrence Phillips) instead of Frerotte.

"We weren't real interested in trading Gus," Washington coach Norv Turner said later. But it was clearly the Rams who cooled on the deal.

The trade would have meant that Shuler had a clear shot at running the team without the constant presence of Frerotte looking over his shoulder. But the coaches seemed to like that competition, and Frerotte's competitiveness. After all, he was the underpaid underdog with nothing to lose, which left Shuler sizzling on a griddle of pressure as the millionaire bonus baby. Not exactly ideal circumstances for a young QB trying to muster the confidence to run a pro team.

Despite being nearly traded, Frerotte headed into training camp in 1996 on equal footing with Shuler as they battled for the starting job. Both showed the typical flaws of young quarterbacks. But the Washington coaching staff decided that Frerotte was making fewer mistakes. Before the season opener, Turner announced that Frerotte had edged Shuler in the competition.

"What I'm looking for is a quarterback who can give us consistency on a week-to-week basis, on a quarter-to-quarter and a play-to-play basis," Turner said.

Shuler thought the decision was hardly fair, but it was a move that many Redskins players had been pushing for all along, mainly because of the coolness Frerotte had showed under fire. At 6-2, 228 pounds, he displayed a linebacker's size and toughness. And he was also down to earth and easygoing, something that Shuler found difficult to be under the circumstances.

Those qualities, Frerotte's play, a rejuvenated offense and a friendly schedule helped the Redskins get off to a 7-1 start in 1996, which did wonders for the team's and the young quarterback's confidence. Shuler could only watch from the bench as Frerotte took over.

"It's just the air about him," Redskins fullback Marc Logan said of Frerotte at the time. "The way he carries himself on and off the field. You have to be intense, but the quarterback has to have a calmness about himself to keep everybody else from being hysterical. And he's got that calmness about him that if things are going tough in the huddle, he can regroup and say, 'Okay, let's roll.'"

Even Shuler had to concede that Frerotte had shown a determination to take over the leadership of the Redskins.

"If things aren't going your way and things are breaking down," Frerotte said, "it's hard to maintain that poise and calm. The guys around you, who know that things are breaking down, they look at you. And if they see you're shaken up, they are going to say, 'I don't know what we're going to do.' But if you have that calm, that steadiness, that poise, those guys are going to be strong, too."

Turner, in particular, wanted a QB with the toughness to get sacked, then get back up and throw a pass on the next play. Many coaches in the league preferred to have their quarterbacks hand off the ball for a running play right after taking a sack, just to make sure their heads are clear, so they won't throw an interception. But Turner, in his experience as an offensive coordinator for the Dallas Cowboys, hated the idea of a sack disrupting the offensive momentum.

In Frerotte, the Redskins coaches realized they had a quarterback determined not to let anything bother him. The tougher the circumstances, the tougher his response. "You gotta just keep coming back from throwing an interception. No matter that you're getting smacked around and it's an exhausting day," he said.

Sonny Jurgenson, the former Redskins quarterbacking great and longtime broadcast color analyst, was another observer who fell in love with Frerotte's style, particularly when he'd get back up off the ground after being sacked and come right back attacking the defense. As a result, Jurgenson took Frerotte under his wing, even inviting him over to his house to view old films of when Jurgy drove the Redskins to sporadic bouts of glory.

"He's kind of an adopted father," Frerotte says of Jurgenson. "We can sit down and talk about anything and everything. He shares a lot with me, and I share a lot with him. For me it's a real treat, because he shares a lot of the moments that he had on the field with me.

"He knows a lot about football. It's changed a little bit since he played. They've changed a lot about the defense. But it's still the same concept.

"When I go to his house, he makes me sit down and watch highlight films from 1961, shows me how he threw this pass early and let the guy run right into it. I just love it. It's a blast."

Frerotte's mindset is definitely throwback, Jurgenson says, beginning with a toughness that Frerotte had acquired growing up in Pennsylvania as a kid who idolized the hard-nosed approach of Terry Bradshaw and the Pittsburgh Steelers.

"When I take a good hit, and I'm getting up slow, sometimes it takes you a few seconds to shake the cobwebs out," Frerotte explains. "One of the things that I notice Coach Turner will do every time I take a good shot, he'll always want me to throw the ball again, drop back and heave it again.

"I love doing that. I love when he does that. A lot of guys will want their coaches to call for a handoff, to let them get back into it. But it doesn't matter if my foot's hurting, my ribs are hurting, or whatever, I'm dropping back and throwing it. It just all goes away. Then you get over to the sideline and it's, 'Aw, man, I didn't know I was hurting that bad.'

"That's the way you have to play... It's just a love of the game."

Another thing that his teammates and coaches liked about Frerotte was his refusal to concede anything to anyone based solely on reputation.

"There's no better feeling than completing a 20-yard route against one-on-one coverage," Frerotte says. "When you go into a game, coaches will be like, 'Maybe we should stay away from this guy today.' I'm like, 'We don't have to stay away from anybody.' If a defensive back is having a good day, we'll find out what kind of day he's having. But even Deion Sanders has

Norv Turner liked Frerotte's style.

his off days. You can't ever just say, 'I'm not going against somebody.'"

He offered perhaps his best display of that toughness in the fourth game of the 1996 season, a victory over the Rams, who were struggling at quarterback and wondering what might have been if they had taken Frerotte in that trade.

Yet, just when things seemed headed even higher at midseason, the team's entire momentum came unraveled with a series of losses. The reversal of fortune was particularly painful in Washington where the fickle fans were frustrated after watching their perennial Super Bowl contender slip into a spiral of losing seasons. Frerotte was all too familiar with the atmosphere. "I went to school in Tulsa," he said. "So I've had many fair-weather fans."

Yet even that couldn't prepare him for the Redskins' dive over the last half of the '96 season. A protracted losing streak dropped them from the top of the NFC East standings right out of the playoff picture.

"We really didn't know what was gonna happen last year," Frerotte explained. "We started out great, then we lose three games by three points. We lose to San Francisco in a tight game. That was probably the best game we played all year.

"But there was a fumble on a kickoff. We thought we had it. Our guy jumps on it, but after everybody gets up from the pile, they have it. Then they go down to kick a field goal...

"That was a heartbreaker. We lost to Arizona a couple of times, one when Boomer Esiason had a career day."

The result was an agony of painfully illustrated lessons for both Frerotte and Shuler. Shuler suffered his in quiet frustration from the bench. He played but one down the entire season. Frerotte's education unfolded on the field, in full public view.

Asked his most important lesson, he answered quickly, "When you have the opportunity you can't let it go by. Every opportunity you have to score or get a first down you have to do it. You're gonna get the ball back, true, but opportunity doesn't happen often when your defense isn't playing well. Every chance you get you really have to go down and try to put some points on the board."

Strangely, they both count among their successes the fact that they faced the circumstances of their competition with class. And despite the awkwardness of it, they remained cordial.

"We were as close as we could be with the competition," Frerotte says.

Shuler immediately saw that as the Redskins began to struggle he would be faced with reporters trying to get him to second-guess the coaching decision to go with Frerotte.

"Every day at my locker they were trying to ask you questions to get you to put your foot in your mouth," Frerotte says. "You just don't let them do that. I told Heath, 'We just can't let them do that. You have to go about it and make sure it's a good thing for us.'"

For the most part, Shuler kept his thoughts to himself and worked with a team-first approach. Later, Frerotte says he told him, "Even though the way it turned out, it might not

Photo by Jim Umphrey

Mike Ditka took over in New Orleans and promptly named Shuler his QB.

be a good thing for you, but it's a good thing for us because we didn't let it go the wrong way."

After the season, Shuler went to the Redskins and restructured his contract so that the club could trade him. The process meant that he risked a good bit of money to gain his freedom. One of the reasons for his anguished mood here at the Quarterback Challenge is that the Redskins and Saints are working out a deal to send him to New Orleans. But the final details of the trade have been stretched out over weeks, meaning that he has been forced to miss a minicamp with new Saints coach Mike Ditka.

Once again, Shuler finds himself twisting in the wind, missing valuable practice time while administrators work out the details.

No wonder he has a low opinion of NFL general managers. Apparently, Shuler also has a low opinion of the new book by New York Jets rookie receiver Keyshawn Johnson, "Just Gimme The Damn Ball."

"What's he done to deserve writing a book?" Shuler asks, ignoring the steak and seafood and good times going on around him at the party.

"Earning your way is definitely a theme in this guy's life," I think, listening to him speak.

Which is good, because's he's about to head into another storm with Ditka and the Saints. The world knows Iron Mike as a quarterback-grinding, egomaniacal kind of guy. He's raving and certified. But the bottom line on Ditka, if you believe all those freaks in Chicago, is about winning and taking responsibility.

"I think it's gonna be a great thing for Heath," Frerotte says. "He's gonna feel very comfortable down there. He's a good quarterback; he's gonna get a shot in New Orleans and he's gonna do well.

"The thing was, this might not have been the offense for him. There might be another offense that's better for you. You look how Brett Favre went from Atlanta to Green Bay. Mark Brunell's the same way (moving from Green Bay to Jacksonville). Everybody moves around until they find their niche. I was lucky enough to come to an offense I was built for."

Ditka certainly seems to treasure Shuler, so much so that in the weeks after the Quarterback Challenge, he completed the trade and promptly released Saints veteran Jim Everett, clearing the way for Shuler to become the starter in New Orleans, a town that was eager to be jolted from the doldrums into a new football life. In fact, some observers, rather tongue-in-cheek, began suggesting that the name of the team be changed to the New Orleans Ditkas. Coach Kielbasa, known for his tendency to rise up on his toes, neck bulging, to go off on some goofball sportswriter in a press conference, invading the land of gumbo? Ain't life strange sometimes?

Lord knows the Saints need him. They were 3-13 in 1996, but forget the record. The pocketbook is where it counts. Game attendance had dropped a couple hundred thousand fannies over the past four miserable seasons.

Over the 1996 offseason, the Saints managed to sell a mere 6,000 season tickets. In the

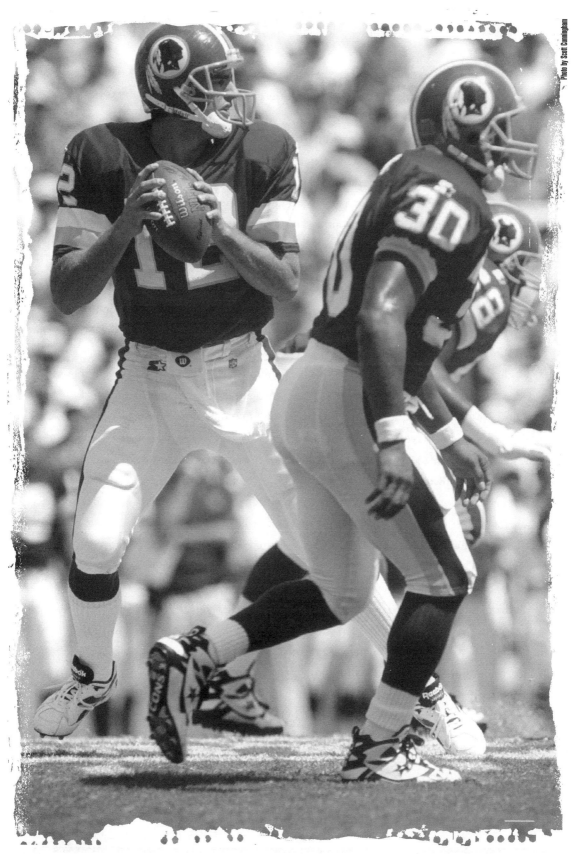

Never mind that Gus was drafted in the seventh round, he came to play in D.C.

first five days after Ditka's hiring, they sold 3,000, with thousands more coming in the weeks afterward.

"We've had a tough couple of years," admitted team marketing director Greg Suit. "Based on early returns, I think Mike is going to stop the bleeding."

To make sure of that, the club followed up the big news of his hiring with a marketing campaign featuring a new slogan: "This year, we're made of iron."

Not exactly. Not yet. It's more like low-grade ore. Even with the smelting that Ditka's furnace can deliver, it'll take some time to shape this club's mettle. Regardless, the place looks like home to Shuler, who is a major part of the team's new look, emphasized by Ditka's willingness to give him a $12 million contract. For certain, the move has brought some raised eyebrows. Everett was a 12-year veteran with 152 NFL starts. Shuler enters his fourth year having started just 13 games.

"I'm very knowledgeable about the game," Shuler says in response.

Just so his $12 million contract doesn't lull Shuler into resting too easy, Ditka drafted Danny Wuerffel, the Heisman Trophy winner who led the University of Florida to a 33-5-1 record. Will Wuerffel's presence give Shuler a dreaded sense of deja vu? Only time will tell.

With Shuler's departure from the Redskins and Frerotte's rise, the process has been completed in a most unusual football story. The last, drafted at no. 197, has unseated the first.

"You're just at a comfort level now," Frerotte says of his promotion and Shuler's departure, "now that you know everything is yours and that if you get hurt somebody else isn't going to come in and take your spot. Now there's a comfort level where you can just go out and play.

"Last year I really tried to put that out of my mind, the idea that if I came out of the game somebody else was going to step in."

He thought a minute after making the statement, realizing that it would be impossible, because in one form or another, there is always a quarterback challenge, always someone waiting on the bench to take your place. In fact, weeks after Shuler's departure, the Redskins traded for Oakland Raiders veteran Jeff Hostetler to serve as Frerotte's backup.

Redskins management had created another challenge, made all the worse by the team's reluctance to give Frerotte a contract worthy of an NFL starter. Finally, after training camp had started, they showed Gus the money, a reported $18 million package making him the highest paid quarterback in franchise history.

Frerotte thought he had been forced to fight a battle in unseating Shuler, but he knew the pressure was right back on. To realize that, all he had to do was look over to the sidelines to see the hypercompetitive Hoss pacing and snorting.

"That's always in the back of your mind," Frerotte acknowledged, "because no matter where you are or who you are, there's always going to be somebody bigger and better who can throw the ball harder and run faster and all of that. I learned last year that every throw means a lot, that you have to work hard every practice and really prepare yourself."

As for Heath Shuler, it occurs to me that he really ought to dance. Life, after all, is short. The beer is cold, the seafood tasty, and that honey of his sure seems to like the Macarena.

Frerotte liked to come back strong after a sack.

Chapter 2/The Next Big Step

Photo by Vernon Biever

Drew drove the Patriots to a Super Bowl date with Green Bay.

t is the summer of Drew Bledsoe's content. Just a few months ago, he reached one of those ultimate levels of accomplishment for a pro quarterback. At the tender age of 24, he directed his New England Patriots to the Super Bowl.

True, Drew and his Patriots lost to the Green Bay Packers in the big game. But in the weeks after the event, Bledsoe encountered what he and his teammates consider to be another incredible piece of good fortune. They were able to jettison the coach, Bill Parcells, who had made life miserable for just about each and every Patriot.

Usually, when a coach gets his team to the Super Bowl that means a big fat contract extension. But Parcells had run afoul of Pats owner Robert Kraft, and the fiery coach had ground down just about all of his relationships with his players. So Parcells moved on to coach the New York Jets, and the Patriots breathed a giant sigh of relief.

"Bill, at times, was a guy who was difficult to play for," Bledsoe says now, acknowledging that he was ready for the coach to go, while still pointing out that without Parcells, the Patriots as a team face a new sort of pressure.

"We as a team have a lot to prove, and I have a lot to prove as a player in that there was a great feeling last year. We got to the Super Bowl last year, and it was Bill vs. the Packers. Basically that was the story. It really was. Without a doubt. As a team, we have to prove that it was the players that made that whole thing happen. I think that feeling is pervasive throughout the entire team."

At the moment, he's in the middle of a photo shoot for the Pinnacle trading card company during Quarterback Challenge week in Orlando. In fact, Bledsoe's trying to fit his substantial head into a helmet for a photo session. The headgear, though, is too small, and the task almost brings tears to his eyes.

"They must have gotten this at a kids' store," Bledsoe mutters as he retracts his head from the tight fit.

The camera guys are snickering about Bledsoe's eyes this morning. He obviously hammered a few during and after last night's quarterback party. Still he's no match for the Packers' Brett Favre, who in addition to staking out a big lead in the race to be the game's next great quarterback, seems to be well on his way to earning a distinction as this generation's Bobby Layne.

While Bledsoe is having trouble getting his head into his hat this morning, friends and teammates say that's not usually the case. First impressions seem to back that up. He has the countenance of a tousle-headed fraternity brother, which helps you to understand why he allows his arm to do much of his talking.

"When he first came into the league, he was such a little kid," says former Patriots offensive lineman Eugene Chung. "You'd look at him and say, 'He's a little kid.' But when you'd see him throw that ball, you'd say, 'Wow! This kid is gonna be a man, a man amongst boys.'

"Sure enough, he's developed into a man. But he's so down-to-earth, that makes it even better, for a guy like him to make the Pro Bowl, year in and year out, being one of the highest paid players in the league. That makes it even better.

"Everytime somebody says, 'Well, Bledsoe gets paid too much,' I tell them, 'You're wrong. You don't know the kid.' He doesn't have a swelled head."

A lot is asked of talented young QBs coming into the league, Chung says. "The crazy thing is that Drew provided it at such a young age. It's gonna be exciting to watch him in future years. He's eventually gonna be in the Hall of Fame, going the way he's going.

"How old is he now? Twenty-three, 24?" Chung asks (Bledsoe has just turned 25) and laughs at the absurdity of someone so young having taken a team to the Super Bowl.

BURNISHED BY BILL

Bledsoe's accomplishments are all the more remarkable considering the gauntlet of hellfire he had to run through to make them happen.

From the very beginning, they were an unlikely pair, a fiftysomething grouch with a bad heart and a twentysomething poster boy with a zillion-dollar arm. Yet, underneath the obvious surface tensions, there was the strongest kind of bond that connected Bledsoe to the crusty, old Bill Parcells.

They needed each other.

Bledsoe, for example, was so impressive in his first two seasons of pro football (in just his second NFL year he threw for a league-leading 4,555 yards) that Parcells figured he required special guidance. Otherwise, he would have been adrift in a world that would give him everything, a world of gladhanders to objectify him and spoil him.

Why, the Boston Pops orchestra even dressed Bledsoe in a tux and put him on stage to read "The Night Before Christmas," just the kind of nonsense that kept Parcells frowning like Scrooge.

"All young men who have adulation poured on them are susceptible," Parcells explained at the time. "Everyone's telling him how great he is. Someone's got to let him know that's not the real world."

Parcells, it seemed, relished being just the person to rain reality all over Bledsoe's parade. For every television analyst pumping grandiose thoughts into the quarterback's ear, for every writer who compared Bledsoe to Dan Marino or some other luminary, for the crowds of New England fans who doted and cooed whenever Bledsoe happened into their midst, Parcells had an answer: A cynical, ego-deflating retort.

"He's not ready for Canton yet," the coach said dryly when reporters got gooey in their praise.

When Bledsoe was named to the Pro Bowl in just his second season, Parcells quipped, "Oh, they must want a very exciting game this year with a lot of interceptions and tipped balls."

If these needles didn't seem to stick, Parcells merely pumped up the volume.

The noise level required some adjustment when Bledsoe arrived in New England four years ago as a $14.5 million rookie out of Washington State.

"You come in here and get Bill Parcells, and he's a loud and overbearing coach," Bledsoe said at the time. "So, at first, when he says something, you kind of clam up... but our relationship is not as one-sided as people think. He'll yell and scream, and I'll talk back to him quietly. I hardly ever yell about anything, so if you see me yelling, you'll know I'm upset. With Bill, yelling is a Jersey thing (Parcells hails from there). I'm from the West Coast. It's just a different way to relate."

Parcells liked to point out that he actually treated Bledsoe much kinder than he treated his former quarterback/whipping boy, Phil Simms, who helped Parcells build two Super Bowl championship teams with the New York Giants.

"Parcells really ground him up," Chung says now of the relationship between the coach and Bledsoe. "He really did. Parcells would grind everyone up, whoever he wanted. He paid a little more attention to Drew because Drew carried that team a lot. Bill really tests your mental toughness, really tests it. He really tries to see whether you crack or not, which I guess is part of being mentally tough.

"He'll break you down and build you up, break you down and build you up," Chung adds. "When he builds you up, your confidence level is unreal. You feel like you can take on the whole world. That's part of Bill's strategy."

The only problem is, that process can eventually wear down relationships, Chung says. "You gotta have some thick skin," he admits.

Parcells said he sensed Bledsoe's father Mac, himself a coach in Washington, understood his approach, but mother Barbara had her doubts.

Playing for his dad, Drew had an idyllic high school career in Walla Walla, where he passed for 2,560 yards and 25 touchdowns as a senior. From there, he became a three-year starter at Washington State before foregoing his senior season to become the top pick in the '93 NFL draft.

It seems that the Bledsoes, who are both English teachers, are so good at turning out bonus babies that they've got another one in production. Drew's younger brother, Adam, established himself as a big, strong-throwing quarterback for Eisenhower High in Yakima. As with Drew, Adam was coached by father Mac, who played at the University of Washington in the '60s.

The New England players weren't unhappy when Bill Parcells jumped to the Jets.

Yet both Bledsoe boys approach football armed with this saying from their parents: Home is where you can go even if you don't throw touchdowns.

With Drew, it didn't seem that haven would ever be needed, but then came his nightmarish third season in the league. Looking back on it, he's ever so thankful that his family was there.

COMPETITION PLUS

Agent Leigh Steinberg likes to point out that, as the top pick in the 1993 draft, Bledsoe had a choice of playing in New England or in Seattle, near his Washington home. Bledsoe chose the Patriots, in part, because he wanted the discipline that playing for Parcells offered.

Not only is Parcells addicted to winning, he's quite good at it. And in the 6-5 Bledsoe, he had the rare, raw quarterbacking talent to win big.

"I tell him he's going to be judged by how his team performs," Parcells said during Bledsoe's early tutelage. "What did his team accomplish while he was the key player? I think that's how we're all judged in athletics. I think he understands that."

The teaming of coach and quarterback brought a dizzying turnaround in the fortunes of the once-awful Patriots, who had just finished a 2-14 season before Parcells drafted Bledsoe in

'93. New England closed out the '94 campaign with a seven-game winning streak to finish 10-6 and earn a wildcard playoff spot, the team's first appearance in the playoffs since 1988.

His teammates were glad to give Bledsoe a hunk of the credit for the finish. "The first time I saw Drew in training camp his rookie year, I knew I'd never played with anyone like him before," said Pats' tight end Ben Coates. "It's his height, and the way he throws the ball so well. His ball really gets up on you fast. He'll hit you in the face mask if you're not careful."

"Drew can throw any kind of pass," agreed former Pats quarterback Steve Grogan. "He reminds me of a young Marino."

Bledsoe's official coming-out party unfolded in a comeback against the Vikings. The Pats had slumped to a 3-6 start to open the '94 season, but Bledsoe and New England's young defense found their maturity in the 11th game of the schedule. They fell behind Minnesota, 20-0, then rallied to win 26-20 in overtime.

On the day, Bledsoe set NFL records for passes and completions, 45 of 70 for 426 yards and three TDs. "Drew kind of took over," said Pats fullback Kevin Turner, who caught the game winner in overtime (during which Bledsoe was six for six).

"It was a good thing for him," Parcells said, "and we needed it badly. After that, we knew we weren't out of any games. It was a tremendous confidence builder.

"A year ago, everybody wanted to know what kind of quarterback he was going to be. I said that we'd find out when he gets knocked down, throws five or six interceptions and is bleeding and hurt, and everybody is on his back. How he responds to that will eventually tell everybody what kind of quarterback he's going to be."

Having found that out, the Patriots chugged on to the playoffs, where, despite his golden arm, Bledsoe threw three interceptions in their first-round playoff loss at Cleveland. "It feels like a disaster," Bledsoe said afterward.

The truth is, it was just the early warning of big trouble.

In the aftermath, replicas of Bledsoe's number 11 jersey appeared in store windows all over New England. Long cool to the Patriots, Boston-area fans fell in love with the team—and Bledsoe.

Boston Globe columnist Bob Ryan even declared that Bledsoe was "becoming the Patriots' answer to Teddy, Bobby and Larry," the famed Boston legends of Williams, Orr and Bird.

Such talk brought cautionary posturing from Parcells. "Does he have the arm to be great? Yes," the coach told reporters. "But there's a lot of guys at the bus station with great arms. Great is a rare quality. We don't have enough evidence yet."

"I wish people would wait until I do something before making these comparisons," Bledsoe agreed, adding. "Our offense needs to cut down on turnovers. Personally, I need to cut down on interceptions."

Overlooked by some was the fact that Bledsoe had thrown 27 that second season, a factor that kept Parcells fussing on the sidelines. But the coach was also very aware that his baby quarterback threw 400 completions, just four shy of the NFL season record held by Warren Moon.

DISASTER

What didn't factor into the equation was Bledsoe's health. He had separated his shoulder the third week of the 1994 season, but played on anyway. Then, in the next to last game of the year, he injured his right shoulder but didn't tell anyone about it, waiting instead for off-season surgery.

The result of the injuries was that Bledsoe altered his throwing mechanics for the '95 season. Suddenly, he was throwing more side-armed and getting balls batted back in his face. He went from being a '94 Pro Bowl selection to the worst-rated passer in the AFC for '95. Even worse, the Pats' record reversed itself, to 6-10, all in the face of giant expectations created by the magical '94 finish and a range of offseason free agent signings.

The plummet was steep, and Bledsoe fell hard, with Parcells leaning on him every day.

"A guy like Bill can be the greatest person to play for or the hardest person to play for," says Chung, now a Green Bay free agent, "and it can be in like a matter of minutes. One minute you love him, the next you wanna go slash his tires... That's how crazy it is."

The edge itself can wear you out, Chung says. "That can really wear down a player, really wear him down."

In addition to Parcells' drive, Bledsoe also had to contend with his own hard-headedness about injury.

"I separated my left shoulder when we were playing the 'Niners (in the third game of the '95 season) and came back and played the rest of that game," he said. "That's the kind of challenge you face. As a player, you have a responsibility to your teammates to try and be on the field as much as you can. So you got to test yourself sometimes.

"That's a message you have to send. Without a doubt, I wanted to stay out there on the field against the 'Niners. To stay on the field just because of that. Because you're a competitor and you want to compete. You want to be in the game and do everything you can to win the game."

COMEBACK

In the wake of the disastrous season, Bledsoe answered the only way he knew how. He knew he needed to work, so he reported early for offseason sessions with Patriots quarterback coach Chris Palmer, a respected teacher.

Together, they began to correct his mechanics difficulties caused by the injuries.

The result of that was a return to the type of performances New England fans had seen in Bledsoe's first two seasons. For '96, he threw for 4,086 yards, 27 TDs, against 15 interceptions.

Pocket Man: Drew looks deep.

After completing just 51 percent of his passes in '95, he charged back, hitting on 59.9 percent of his tosses.

The numbers alone, however, don't tell the story of yet more bumpy terrain.

"Last season kind of encapsulated a career really," Bledsoe says after finishing the photo shoot, "because there were some severe ups and downs in the whole thing.

"I think the most important thing for a quarterback is that you have to be able to continue to perform at a consistent level, regardless of whether you just threw five picks or just threw four touchdowns. You gotta be able to come back and play the next play like nothing's happened the play before. That's a battle that you gotta fight in your head throughout the season, throughout games..."

Without a doubt, the biggest down came just when he and his teammates figured they were about to emerge.

"We played Denver last year in the middle of the season in a game that really was billed as the battle of the two top teams in the AFC," he says. "It was hyped as all that, and we were jacked up for the game. But we just got worked over by the Broncos. It was like 38-6, or something like that. After that game, you just felt sick because everything you worked so hard for all of a sudden was just put right back in your face."

The Super Bowl loss wasn't quite the same downer, mostly because getting there was such a reward. But it was a downer all the same, Bledsoe says.

"You get there to that game, and there's nothing more in the world you want than to win that game. And it's just a huge, huge letdown when you lose that game.

"After being away from football for a month or two and being able to gain a little perspective, I can look back and say, 'Okay, it was a successful season. We won a lot of games and made it to the Super Bowl.' But at the same time, in your gut, you always feel like, 'Geez, we left something there that we could have taken.'"

All of which has him eager to get back at it, especially now that he won't have to take those sideline cowhidings and slow walks with Parcells.

"Yeah, yeah. I am looking forward to it," Bledsoe says. "I, myself, and our team as a whole have a lot to prove, now that Bill is gone. We gotta prove that we accomplished something on the field last year that we can duplicate or improve on without Bill's help."

Still, there's little question that Parcells was a driving force in the equation. The question now is, just how much of a force was he? Will new coach Pete Carroll find a kinder, gentler way to push this young team back to the top?

"We can work real hard and enjoy the work," Carroll has promised his players.

"Pete is different from Bill, but not as different as people would think," Bledsoe said. "He's positive and upbeat, so his personality is somewhat different. But Pete is also a hard-driving guy. He just does it in a different way. He's got us working hard, as hard or harder than Bill worked us, but it just feels different because of the way that he approaches things.

"I'm glad I had the opportunity to play for Bill. Bill is one of the most successful coaches in the history of the NFL. But I'm also excited about the opportunity to move on to a new era in my career and in the Patriots' life."

Having made this break, Bledsoe knows the pressure will be immense, but he says that he welcomes all of it, because that's what a competitor is supposed to do, supposed to love to do.

"It's unbelievable," he says of that pressure. "There's such emotional highs and lows, such dramatic changes that happen, that you've got to keep a perspective."

Despite his age, Drew Bledsoe is somebody who now knows all about perspective. If nothing else, Bill Parcells has made sure of that.

Chapter 3/Still Slingin

f you drive to Sweetwater, which is a few hours west of Dallas, and head up to Rotan, which is a little town north of Sweetwater, then press on into Stonewall County until you cross the Brazos River, you'll find Double Mountain rising out of the West Texas plain. There, at the foot of the mountain, is the Bar Lazy S Ranch, home for the past half century of Slingin' Sammy Baugh, Hall of Fame quarterback, retired cowboy, world-class cusser and honest-to-goodness shiznit.

Slingin' Sammy was a triple threat shiznit in the 1940s.

Now 80-something, Baugh's knees are too brittle for roping calves. He gave that up in his 60s, and he finally quit riding horses in his 70s, about the same time that he began turning over his 7,500-acre ranch to his children. These days Baugh spends his time playing golf, watching televised sports, and reading about Indians (like Heath Shuler, he's part Cherokee). He also likes chewing tobacco and spitting into a plastic cup.

The golf is great exercise for an old man, he says. "It's not hard because you walk to the ball, hit the damn thing, and then go look for it."

The cussing he reserves mostly for reminiscing about his football days. A few years back when a TV crew came to his ranch to film his recollections for the 75th anniversary of pro football, Baugh warned them, "I'm gonna swear. Don't come down here if you don't want to hear swearin'."

True to his word, he swore up a storm, but the producers of the show didn't edit any of the cusswords out. To have done that would have been a denial of the game's true nature.

His language, after all, is locker room talk, sort of a jock poetry, steeped in Texas football tradition, where all the opponents are SOBs and the adjectives seldom run more than four letters. The leather-helmeted football he played was a tough game; it required tough men who spoke a tough language.

Sam Baugh, to borrow from his own parlance, was one of the toughest sumbitches around.

He played in the days of limited substitution rules, when the game belonged to the players, who had to think on their feet. On offense, he played quarterback (halfback in the single wing); on defense, he played safety; on special teams, he did the punting. When he got sacked on third down (there were no early whistles to protect quarterbacks in the old days), he had to pick himself up off the ground and boom off a punt. Then he had to hustle downfield to play defense. All of this he did in premier fashion.

In 1936, he led Texas Christian to a Sugar Bowl win over LSU. The next year, 1937, he quarterbacked the Horned Frogs to victory in the first Cotton Bowl. That summer he carried a group of college all-stars to a 7-0 win, a major upset, over the NFL champion Green Bay Packers. In his rookie NFL season that fall, he took the upstart Washington Redskins to the league championship.

In the 1937 title game against the Chicago Bears on ice-glazed Soldier Field, rookie Baugh completed 17 of 34 passes for 352 yards and three touchdowns, an incredible feat for that era. He did this while playing the full 60 minutes of the game, every offensive and defensive play.

Bronko Nagurski, the great Bears fullback, had one assignment that day. "In that game I was playing safety," Baugh recalls, "and when Bronko would break through a hole, no matter where I was, he'd come right to me. I bet you I knocked him down seven times in that ball game. I got to where I wouldn't try to tackle him. I'd block him down on that ice. I'd hit him and he'd lose his footing.

"After the game I asked him why he kept coming after me. He said, 'I'll tell you why. I was supposed to run over you and get you out of the game.'"

When Baugh came to the NFL in 1937, pro football was largely a ground game, dominated by single-wing and short punt formations. But he was the forerunner of the modern, high-tech passing quarterback, and he lorded over the game's transition to the T-formation offense. Over 16 NFL seasons, he threw for more than 22,000 yards, and six times led the league in passing, while seemingly setting yardage records every year.

In one game against Detroit in 1943, he threw four touchdown passes and as a safety made four interceptions. That year, he led the league in both touchdown passes (23) and interceptions made (11), the only player to ever do so. His 1945 quarterback rating, 109.9, remains one of the highest in league history.

As a punter, he liked to angle his low, long kicks for the sideline, which made a runback all but impossible. Four times he led the NFL in punting, and in 1940, he averaged 51.3 yards per punt, a record that remains unbroken.

With "hang time" the emphasis for today's punters, a kicker like Baugh might never get a chance in the modern game. But he says the real way to control a game by kicking is to pick the spot on the sideline and hit it.

"The only time I kicked down the center of the field," he says, "was if we thought the return man was a fumbler."

Baugh says the crucial phase of his quarterbacking development came at TCU, where legendary coach Dutch Meyer entrusted him to run a wide-open passing attack. "We had what you call the short passing game," Baugh says. "From what you hear today, you'd think that the San Francisco 49ers invented it or something."

Meyer told his young quarterback he could throw anywhere on the field, any time he wanted, to any receiver he wanted.

"We had a spread formation, which a lot of teams then didn't have. We played a wide-open brand of football at TCU. That helped me more than anything," Baugh says.

He was surprised, upon arriving in Washington for his first season of pro ball, to find the offense so conservative. Soon, however, the rookie had convinced his coaches to open up the game. When that change resulted in a championship for the young team, it seemed like the Redskins might come to dominate the league.

But then Baugh watched in amazement over the ensuing months as Redskins owner George Preston Marshall disassembled their championship team. Baugh had signed out of TCU for the overwhelming sum of $12,000 for his first season (and was soon making $20,000 per year).

But the rest of the club made far less. Only three players earned $2,750 per season. The rest were paid $150 per game or less. One of the three "highly paid" players was running back Cliff Battles, out of West Virginia Wesleyan, who had led the NFL in rushing during the championship season. He had also scored on three long touchdown runs during a key road game against the New York Giants.

"The next year in training camp, Battles wanted a $250 raise, to $3,000 per season," Baugh recalled. "Marshall wouldn't give it to him."

They wrangled over money until Battles finally quit and took a job at Columbia University as a backfield coach. He never played pro ball again.

"You tell people that this day and time, they can't believe it," Baugh says. "He wanted $250 more and couldn't get it. Hell, that son of a bitch led the league in rushing; he was a great pass receiver; he played good defense."

Marshall, who owned a chain of laundries, had just moved the team to Washington after a miserable first season in Boston. He squeezed player salaries.

"Shit," Baugh recalls. "He did some of the craziest goddam things. The sportswriters, everybody, hated the son of a bitch before it was all over. He was a smart businessman. But if a good football player would ask for more money than Marshall thought he was worth, he'd get rid of him just like that.

"We had a damn good tackle named Fred Davis out of Alabama, one of the best in the league. He played for us three seasons and wanted a little more than he was making. Marshall got rid of him in the next three or four days, sent him to the Bears for a goddam back that never helped us a lick. Marshall just gave Davis to the Bears, and we had to play against him.

Davis had knocked-out teeth, and he always took his fake teeth out before a game. He'd just have gums. When we played the Bears, I'd line up behind center and look over the line at Fred, and he'd just be grinning at me. We'd snap the ball, and goddam, here he'd come.

"I tell you he was tougher than a f——— boot. He just relished knocking my ass off because he knew Mr. Marshall would be watching."

Despite the diminished roster, the Redskins managed to return to the league championship game in 1940. Two weeks before the season ended, they beat the Bears, 7-3, and afterward Marshall told reporters that the Chicago players were "quitters." When the two teams met for the title, Bears coach George Halas read Marshall's newspaper clippings to his players, who then went out and greased the 'Skins, 73-0, in Washington.

"We had one of the best teams we ever had," Baugh recalls. "That was just a game where we didn't hit a lick, and Mr. Marshall had given the Bears plenty of motivation. They were on our 2- or 3-yard line when the game was over, getting ready to score again."

In 1942 and '43, the Bears and 'Skins again played for the title. Baugh tossed a 39-yard scoring pass to give Washington the '42 championship, 14-6. The next year the Bears won, 41-21.

Perhaps Baugh's strangest title game came in 1945, against the Cleveland Rams. Always a gambler, he was throwing a pass out of his own end zone when the ball struck the goal post cross bar and bounced out of bounds in the end zone.

Under an obscure rule at the time, the play was ruled a safety. The rule was later changed, but the two points gave the Rams the championship, 15-14.

"I tried to throw between the goal posts and hit the damn cross bar," Baugh says, laughing. "That's what lost us the game. I didn't even know the rule was in there until it happened. I don't think it had ever happened before."

The loss capped a season in which Baugh had completed 70.3 percent of his passes, the second-highest rated passing season in NFL history.

BASEBALL

People assume that Baugh earned his nickname in football, but a Fort Worth sportswriter tagged Baugh "Slingin' Sammy" after watching him play third base at TCU.

In fact, Baugh signed a big-league contract with the St. Louis Cardinals organization, and for three seasons played pro baseball in the summer and pro football in the winter. His experiences there afforded him a chance to play against a Negro League all-star team led by Cool Papa Bell. Unfortunately, the game ended "in the damndest riot I've ever seen," he says.

But Baugh's best baseball story comes from a minor league game in Columbus, Ohio: "We were playing Milwaukee [then a minor league city] in Columbus, and they had a ballplayer there named Ted Williams, a young boy, about 17. He played right field, and he could hit the hell out of that damn ball. Wham!

"I never will forget that son of a bitch would go out in right field and stick his damn glove in his back pocket. He'd turn his back on the pitcher on the mound getting ready to throw. Williams would be out there in right field taking exercise, doing jumping jacks.

"There were some old ballplayers on our team coming back down from the big league. His exercising would make these old ballplayers cuss. 'Goddam,' they'd say. 'That damn bushleaguer. They ought to send him back down. Get him out of here!'

"They hated Ted Williams. Here was a young rookie who didn't give a f—- about anything. Nothing bothered him. He'd be out there exercising, but when the pitcher would throw, he'd be back around there with his glove on and be ready if he had to go get the ball.

"Then he'd come to the plate and wham! He'd knock a goddam board off the fence in the outfield when he hit the ball. I always wondered how that Milwaukee manager put up with that. I guess he was told to by the ones above. Williams was a screwball in a lot of ways, really. I thought he'd change when he got up to Boston. But I don't think he ever did."

Baugh, himself, tore his sternum playing in a football exhibition game after the 1937 championship, which hampered his baseball development the next spring. He never made it to the big leagues.

But he chugged on in football to become a charter inductee into the Hall of Fame. The last half of his career the Redskins had sorry teams, and he spent his years perfecting the dodge of an oncoming rush and throwing on the run. He hated the muggy city of Washington and always went straight to his ranch the day the season ended. Still, he remained fiercely loyal to the Redskins.

His Native American heritage wasn't offended by the team's name, he says. "I always considered it an honor."

After his playing career ended in 1952, he went on to coach 16 seasons. Occasionally someone would talk him into a head coaching job, but mostly he just wanted to be an assistant. That way, he was free to go back to his beloved ranch in the offseasons. In his 40s, he took up calf-roping competition on the cowboy circuit.

Today his fun comes on the golf course. His wife of many years, Edmonia, died a few years back, and now Baugh has time on his hands. He'll be happy to tee it up with you if you're passing through Rotan. Just don't listen to his talk about not being able to play worth a damn.

The skinny on his game in West Texas is that he whips people half his age.

"Old time smashmouth football."

Chapter 4/Brett Favre
From Very Big Thrills To Jagged Little Pills... And Back Again

Photo by Tim Doughrey

Brett can scoot when he needs to, but his arm is more dangerous.

The shame of it all for Brett Favre, was that he had to start all over again in the testy business of proving himself. Just when he had established that he could overcome being a no-name kid from Mississippi, that he could survive an auto wreck that nearly killed him, that he could stand in the face of bone-crushing pass rushes week after week to deliver the Green Bay Packers from the realm of also-rans and doormats into the elite air of championship contenders. . .

Just when he had all those Cheeseheads idolizing his cocksure image, the power of his classic quarterback pose, his head encased in that indestructible plastic Packer gold, his gaze directed upfield, the ball, clutched sternum high, loaded in his mitts like a bullet. Just when he had all of this, Brett Favre had to go and get real.

It was in May 1996 that Favre, the Most Valuable Player of the NFL, announced that he had become addicted to the painkiller Vicodin, those little pills they gobble in NFL locker rooms when they don't have time for the pain. Following his announcement, he quickly retreated to a treatment facility in Topeka, Kansas, where he would spend 46 days getting his appetites under control. Favre had started 63 consecutive regular-season games for the Packers and had become known as the kind of guy who refused to let injury keep him from playing.

The announcement shocked the sports world, just as it shocked many of his teammates and people in the Packer organization. Yes, it was best for him to come clean, but the fans would have preferred that it just hadn't happened, because they like their sports heroes suitable for framing and mythologizing. They like their heroes without encumbrances. O.J. without the white Bronco. Pete Rose without the bookie's private number.

Okay, so Brett Favre proved to be very different from them. He admitted his addiction to painkillers and sought help for it. Not only that, he made it hard on himself by submitting to NFL supervision on the matter, rather than skating by on the sly with private treatment. That meant the NFL could test him weekly if it wanted, that he wouldn't be able to slink past the situation without confronting his troubles.

THE FALL

In disclosing the circumstances, Favre said he knew he had a problem in the spring of 1996 when he had a seizure at a hospital after undergoing offseason ankle surgery. The announcement generated substantial speculation that Favre also had an alcohol problem, but he said his difficulties were limited to the use of painkillers.

At the time, Favre dared anyone who doubted him to bet against him. Neither his team nor his teammates did. In fact, Packer officials predicted that Favre would be ready for the opening of Packers training camp by July 15. Sure enough, he was.

That almost made his recovery sound simple, but the issue was far from that. The NFL is a brutal business, especially for quarterbacks, especially for quarterbacks like Favre. He's a guy with a warrior mentality and a 50-caliber arm, which means that he won't back down from the enemy, and because he's so dangerous, the enemy can't afford to back down from him. Sunday after Sunday, opponents have brought the big rush at him, and playmaker that he is, Favre has stood in the face of those rushes, testing the circumstances, waiting 'til the last possible instant—before everything crashes down on him—to make something happen.

BRAVEHEART

"It would mean everything to bring the Packers back to the Super Bowl. That's what I'm living for," Favre had said earlier in the year, well before he acknowledged his problem. "And there's no doubt that before my career is over—it may not be this year—I'm going to win a Super Bowl in Green Bay. And it'll be like no other."

The phrase jumped at you from right out of the quote.

That's what I'm living for.

Brett Favre wanted to win in the worst possible way, and that very hypercompetitiveness was what set him apart. It was also the thing that could have gotten him killed, dead of a stroke caused by overdependence on painkillers.

Why? Because he wanted to win. Because that's what we expect from our champions. They have to be someone willing to lay it all on the line, someone who wants each win in the worst possible way, someone willing to find a way to play through the pain.

The situation wasn't the first time that one of our sports heroes has taken us to the dark recesses, the outer reaches, of desire. But Favre was so young and driven, so charismatic, so fresh-faced, so unlike Lyle Alzado.

In fact, his appeal began with his improbable journey from the University of Southern Mississippi (which explains the nickname "Country" bestowed upon him by his Packer team-mates) to NFL stardom. At Southern Miss, Favre rose to prominence by leading his underdog team to a series of wins over Florida State, Alabama and other college football powerhouses.

But his reputation as a gritty kid with a big gun was diminished when he suffered serious injuries in an auto accident just before his senior year, which required the removal of nearly two feet of his intestine. The subsequent surgeries and recovery complications would play a part in his growing dependence on painkillers.

The Atlanta Falcons took him in the second round of the 1991 draft (33rd overall) and promptly gave him the standard rookie treatment—a third-string status and a seat on the bench his first season.

Favre, however, had impressed Packer executive Ron Wolf with his performance at Southern Miss, so Green Bay plunked down a first-round draft pick to obtain him in February 1992. As the teams wrapped up the trade, Falcons personnel director Ken Herock phoned Wolf and told him, "I just made you Executive of the Year."

The Packers had former San Francisco 49ers offensive coordinator Mike Holmgren as their coach, and they thought Favre would be a nice backup to starter Don Majkowski. In time, they figured the 6-2, 230-pound Favre would be the main guy to throw the ball in those famous 49er-style slants and crossing patterns.

That schedule was pushed a bit when Majkowski got injured early in the '92 schedule, and Favre stepped in with the kind of year that coaches dream of getting out of a second-year quarterback, finishing with 302 completions for 3,227 yards and 18 TDs. Holmgren, who had worked with Joe Montana and Steve Young in San Francisco, said Favre easily had the strongest arm he had ever seen on a QB.

Amazed at his performance, reporters asked Favre for an assessment. "I have a pretty strong arm and I throw downfield a lot," he replied. "I use a lot of three-step drops. I throw some play action and do move around. I'm not the most accurate passer, but I'm usually close enough."

"He's going to be great," predicted receiver Mark Clayton.

The huge negative, obviously, was the lack of discipline and self-control. What he possessed, though, was an incredible capacity for improvisation.

Caught in a trap? "Don't worry, Coach," Favre would say. "I'll shake loose and make things happen."

Holmgren spent too many frustrating afternoons trying to make Favre understand that sometimes he just had to throw the damn ball away. "Sure," Favre would say on the sidelines.

Then he'd go back in, get trapped, and still send the ball upfield into a crowd on a wing and a prayer that his arm strength and boyish luck would make something happen.

The circumstances explained how Favre threw a league-leading 24 interceptions in '93 and fumbled 14 times, providing fodder for critics' charges that he was excitable and prone to mistakes. But the Packers showed their regard by subsequently shipping Majkowski, once a local hero, to Indianapolis and signing "Country" to a five-year contract worth about $20 million before the 1994 season.

Yet early in the '94 campaign, an exasperated Holmgren was still considering benching Favre in favor of backup Mark Brunell.

"Oh, we had a wonderful adjustment period there," Holmgren says now. "Brett was this wild stallion. I admit I was harder on him than I have been on any quarterback I've ever coached."

That included whacking him upside the helmet when talking didn't seem to work. "I coached him like other coaches coach linebackers," Holmgren admitted.

Somewhere early in the 1994 schedule, Favre finally got the message. Holmgren says that he and the quarterback finally figured the whole thing out.

"I'm average in smarts," Favre once appraised. "But in ability I'm pretty good."

He confirmed that in '94 by turning in a stellar season (3,882 yards, 38 TDs, 14 INTs) and leading the Packers to a wild-card playoff slot. The cap to an outstanding regular schedule was his last-second diving touchdown against the Falcons, assuring Green Bay of a spot in the playoffs.

"I was pretty confident," Favre said of the final drive. "I kept telling the guys on the sideline that we were going to score, that someone was going to make a play. I just didn't think it would be me."

Next in the storybook was Green Bay's first-round win over Detroit in the 1994 playoffs. After that, the Packers' season ended with a loss in Dallas, but Favre had established the teamwide confidence for an outstanding 1995 season.

Despite losing primary target Sterling Sharpe to a career-ending injury, Favre threw for a league-leading 4,413 yards and 38 touchdowns against only 13 interceptions in 1995. Then he saved his best performance for the divisional playoffs while leading the Packers to a 27-17 upset of the defending Super Bowl champion 49ers.

Favre fired 21 completions in 28 attempts for 299 yards and three touchdowns, a showing that elevated the Packers to the NFC championship game against the Dallas Cowboys, a level of competiton Green Bay teams hadn't reached since the Super Bowl championship teams of Vince Lombardi.

"Beating the 49ers is about the biggest win I ever had," Favre said. "I didn't really think about my numbers at the time, though, because we beat them so easily. It really didn't sink in 'til later."

Favre's da bomb!

Although the Packers got off to a slow start in the NFC title match with Dallas, Favre settled down and drove his team to the verge of what appeared to be a go-ahead score. Instead, he threw an interception that allowed the Cowboys to win, 38-27.

"If I don't throw that interception to Larry Brown late in the fourth quarter, we win that game," he said afterward. "We had been scoring at will in the second half, and if we had scored again I think it would have driven a stake through their hearts because they'd never been in that position before."

Despite the defeat, Favre and his Packers had climbed the mountain, and the view from the top had told them they could compete. For three seasons, the pressure to take them there had been Favre's because the entire Green Bay offense was built around his quarterback play. Being named the league's MVP only added to his confidence and the fans' expectations that bigger things were ahead.

In the face of all that momentum, he stepped back to confront his addiction, all the while very aware that if he faltered coming out of treatment, the entire Packer machine would probably come to a halt.

His supporters pointed out that Favre mostly relied on the painkillers to get him through the achy days after games, not the games themselves. For his teammates and family, there was the matter of his competitive history. His rise to prominence had been a short, brilliant trip, which created hope that his return would follow a similar route.

His path, however, was lined with a number of skeptics, not so much people critical of Favre as they were simply aware of the real dangers and impossibilities of drug addiction. They were waiting to see if he really was willing to live for that day when Green Bay returned to the Super Bowl.

To his credit, Favre didn't keep anyone in suspense. He came out of treatment and headed right into training camp, building confidence in those around him from the very start.

Regardless, it was not an easy journey. The ensuing months also brought the arrest of his 19-year-old sister Brandi in connection with a drive-by shooting (she was not accused of being the trigger person and later received a year's probation in connection with the incident), but worse, Favre's 29-year-old brother, Scott, was charged with felony drunk driving following a wreck that killed a close family friend.

The incidents and their subsequent publicity tormented Favre, who comes from a close family in the hamlet of Kiln (pronounced Kill) in Mississippi. At nearby Hancock Central High, Irvin Favre spent 30 years coaching football, a tenure that saw him direct all three of his sons, Scott, Brett and Jeff, as quarterbacks. Mom Bonita was a special education teacher.

"Leave my family out of it," Favre told reporters who asked about his brother and sister. "How would you like it if something happened to one of your family members and you'd see it on the front page of every newspaper in the United States? It's not fair to them.

"They enjoy watching me play pro football. They enjoy every honor I ever won. But they don't enjoy the other side of it, as I don't enjoy it."

His personal problems were accompanied by a host of on-field hurdles. Primary receiver Robert Brooks was lost to a knee injury, soon to be followed by wideout Antonio Freeman with a broken arm and tight end Mark Chmura with a torn arch.

Not only was the receiving corps in turmoil, the offensive line was in shreds. Veteran left tackle Kent Ruettgers, Favre's primary guardian, missed most of the season with a degenerative knee condition that finally forced his retirement, leaving a mish-mash of rookie John Michels, third-year understudy Gary Grown and journeyman Bruce Wilkerson.

The patchwork contributed to Favre being sacked a career-high 40 times over the 1996 season, all with no painkillers to help him overcome the plethora of aches that resulted from being slammed to the ground week after week.

"It was like, 'OK, if it wasn't tough enough on you to start the season, let's make it a little tougher,'" Favre would later explain. "'We'll take Robert out. Ruettgers is not going to be back, and that's the most important position on the offense. Then along the way, we'll take your No. 2 receiver out.' It was like, 'OK, we'll put you to the test and see how you respond.'"

The numbers indicate the intensity with which he met the challenge. He threw for 3,899 yards over 16 regular-season games and an NFC-record 39 touchdowns, breaking his own record of 38 set in '95. This stunning productivity drove the Packers to a 13-3 regular season and a playoff march that resulted in the club's first Super Bowl victory in three decades.

"Coming into the season, I really wanted to prove to people that it really wasn't that I was back," Favre said on the eve of the Super Bowl. The reason for that, was that he believed he never really left.

The source of Favre's statement was his great pride in showing up every Sunday. At season's end, he had started 77 consecutive regular-season games (86 including the playoffs) for his team.

"The quarterback is supposedly someone who doesn't want to get hit," said Robert Brooks. "But Brett is one of the toughest guys on the team. To know that your leader can endure punishment and not miss games, it gives you a sense of confidence."

"He's Superman," agreed receiver Andre Rison.

There was little question that with two consecutive league MVP awards and the championship — not to mention his victory over himself — Favre had become the game's dominant player.

San Francisco quarterback Steve Young admitted that up until a couple of years ago he was still offering Favre advice. Now, Young said, he sits back and takes note of things in the Packer QB's approach, looking for things that will help his own game.

However, Favre's instincts, his ability to look into the chaos on the field and find options just as the world is about to collapse, those are gifts impossible to duplicate.

"That's what separates him right now," Young said of Favre, "the plays that he's making out of the pocket. If Mike Holmgren were gonna script it, there'd be no way. And Mike knows it. So there's a huge onus on Brett to do that every week.

"That's a huge responsibility, to say, 'We have no plan for you, Brett, but you gotta make six or seven plays today.' That's a huge responsibility."

One that Favre seems very eager to shoulder. Best of all, he's now willing to live for it.

Chapter 5/Always Monkey Time

Photo by Tim Humphrey

Young plays the game like a free safety.

Here we are at yet another interview session during the Quarterback Challenge weekend. This time the subject is the San Francisco 49ers' Steve Young, and this time the proceedings will be amazingly cordial. How do I know this? Because Steve Young has walked into his photo shoot for Pinnacle Trading Cards humming Sheryl Crow's "Every Day Is A Winding Road."

At last year's QB Challenge, it seems, some of the writers slipped up and mentioned the dreaded M-word, prompting Young to overheat in a hurry and fuss at the group. "Why are you guys always bringing up Montana?" he asked angrily, which was way out of tenor for this low-key affair. Young, you see, had thought that he put the Montana issue to rest a few years earlier, meaning that reporters would no longer ask him questions about Super Joe.

You might recall the urge to be mischievous that overcame Young in the final delicious minutes of his team's Super Bowl XXIX blowout of the San Diego Chargers in January 1995. Able to contain himself no longer, Young turned to a group of his teammates and asked, "Someone take the monkey off my back, please!"

The monkey, of course, was the considerable legend of former San Francisco quarterback Joe Montana, who had led the 'Niners to four Super Bowl titles in the 1980s.

Young's difficulty in following Montana's brilliant act was well-documented at the time. For three straight seasons, Young had led the NFL in passing, but each of those three seasons the 49ers had fallen in the playoffs. San Francisco fans, religious in their worship of Montana, had long concluded that Young didn't have the special magic to lead "Joe's team" to the title.

Finally, however, after a season of unprecedented brilliance, Young had accomplished just that. And even before the game was over, even before his MVP award and the league championship trophy had been presented, Young was eager to be relieved of his burden.

Volunteering to do the honors, offensive tackle Harris Barton stepped up and grabbed the imaginary primate and ripped it off as Young laughed with delight.

"That thing was a gorilla," Barton announced. "It's gone forever."

It was a touching, defining moment for Young, yet all the same, it was patently false. Steve Young will never be free of the shadow of Joe Montana. If anything, Young's driving the 49ers to a Super Bowl victory only drew the two quarterbacks closer as the members of a very small, very exclusive fraternity, one in which Montana has been elected president for eternity and Young will always be the driven, unheralded pledge.

"Young won a Super Bowl in his only try, but he's still three behind Montana, and no one seriously believes he will ever catch up," wrote *San Francisco Chronical* columnist Ira Miller at the start of the '95 season, an attitude shared by many 49er fans.

There could be worse fates, of course. Young could be one of the many lesser quarterbacks who could never measure up. Instead, he has shown the talent and drive to survive the withering pressure of Montana's legend. Just don't make the mistake of asking him about it.

This year, the writers at the QB Challenge are careful to avoid any mention of Monkey Montana, and Young rewards them with a laid-back interview. He even admits that he no longer begrudges autograph hounds. In the past, he used to try to figure out which ones were trying to make money and which ones were just fans hungry for a signature.

"I don't fight it as much as I used to," he says. "I don't worry if it's adults or kids. I used to try to figure out who was selling, who was buying. Who cares? Who cares? If someone wants to make a buck, don't wear yourself out worrying about it."

He says this as if it has taken some effort to convince himself of this position. Then again, that's a common process for Young. For example, he says he has kept few mementos and memorabilia from his glory years. Early in his career, he says, he decided that he either had to collect everything or pretend he didn't care about any of it. So he chose to pretend he didn't care.

Just like he's pretending now that he's not consumed by the idea of spending his life in Montana's shadow or that he really doesn't mind signing autographs for the unwashed masses.

The one thing he does admit to treasuring is his jersey from that glorious Super Bowl afternoon, only he says he can't remember where it is in the stacks of stuff around his house. "Everything else is somewhere," he says of his haphazardly organized residence. "I just don't know where."

"You really don't know where it is?" a writer asks.

"I know," Young says, effectively admitting that he was pretending about this, too.

Which left me to wonder, how does he keep all of this pretending straight? It also occurs to me that just being Steve Young and keeping track of all this pretending must be a fairly complicated proposition.

FRUSTRATION

The seasons since his hour of glory have been frought with injury and frustration for the soon-to-be-36-year-old Young. He has missed all or part of 14 games the past two years. In 1995, he was forced to seek midseason shoulder surgery in hopes of making the playoffs. A year later it was two concussions, a groin pull and finally broken ribs that did him in.

"If you're not healthy, like I wasn't the last two years, then you put yourself in a real jam," Young says, acknowledging that the challenge for 1997 will be showing that he can sustain the impact of 16 games and the playoffs.

The circumstances have led to questions about his plans for retirement. "I haven't really gotten to the point where I'm thinking about it," he says, "so I guess that's a good sign. I'd like to put a few years of health together and get back to where I was a few years ago."

Strangely, even in the down times, he encounters Montana's shadow. After all, didn't Super Joe return from a potentially career-ending back injury to lead the 'Niners to a championship?

If there has been any consolation during Young's time on the injured list, it has been the good feelings left over from his 1994 performance, perhaps the best ever for a quarterback. He threw 35 touchdown passes and had a .703 completion percentage, good enough for a 112.8 QB rating, all team records, all better than Super Joe. Then Young capped off the season by throwing for a record six touchdowns and 325 yards in the Super Bowl (and rushing for another 49).

With the breakthrough, the season brought two emotional releases for Young. First came his celebratory jaunt around Candlestick Park, during which he unforgettably bowled over a television cameraman, after the 49ers' victory over the Dallas Cowboys in the National Football Conference championship game.

But the most emotional moment by far came in the San Francisco dressing room after the Super Bowl as Young held the MVP trophy aloft. "There were times it was dark, really dark," he told his teammates. "But you guys really made a commitment. This is all a part of yours. This is the greatest feeling in the world. No one can ever. . . Ever. . . Ever. . . Take it away from us. Ever!!!"

Young had also won the passing title for a fourth straight season, bringing his rating those four seasons to 106.2.

In his best four campaigns, Montana could compile a rating no higher than 102.4.

The game, however, is not about ratings. It's about championships.

"I think Joe is the greatest, and I think Steve can become one of the great players in that category," former 49ers coach Bill Walsh, the man who drafted Montana and traded for

Young, said as the '95 season opened. "Steve is right at that juncture in his career."

Sure enough, he began the '95 season on the same tare. He lost his headgear in a preseason game against San Diego, yet fearlessly ran helmetless with the ball for a gain. In his first three regular-season games he passed for 875 yards and eight touchdowns (against two interceptions) with a 70.6 completion percentage. He also ran for 120 yards on 18 carries, making him the team's second-leading ground gainer.

Then came the shoulder injury against Indianapolis in October, and like that, he was out of the Super Joe sweepstakes. The setback broke his league-best streak of starting 62 straight games, during which the 49ers had rung up a 47-15 record, including 5-2 in the playoffs.

Used to his hardnosed style, the San Francisco media compared Young to Evel Knievel and predicted he would be back by the Dallas Cowboys game November 12. Young was in uniform on the bench, but the Monday after San Francisco's exhilirating upset, the team announced that Young would need surgery in order to be ready for the playoffs.

Without a doubt, it was the most physically challenging time in his career, Young says now. "I had to play three games in the middle of the season, basically just kind of waving my arm around. I couldn't lift it very well and I was trying to play, and I thought to myself, 'It's hard enough trying to play in this league, let alone not being able to play to your ability.' That was very frustrating."

Whether he could make it back was anyone's guess, but reporters in the Bay area had learned not to bet against him.

"Young'll sleep when he's dead," quipped *San Francisco Examiner* columnist Ray Ratto.

Young made it back in '95, only to see his team suffer a disappointing defeat to Green Bay in the NFC playoffs. For 1996, he managed to rack up his fifth NFL passing title in six years, despite the series of injuries, by rolling up a 97.1 QB rating and throwing for better than 2,400 yards. He was also sacked 34 times, however, and when it came time to meet the Packers again in the playoffs, Young was trying to fight through the pain of broken ribs. He played only one ineffective series as the Packers rolled past the Niners on the way to the Super Bowl.

"That wasn't even close," he said of the Packer game. "That was take 15 aspirin and see what you can do. Fortunately, it wasn't the broken ribs that hurt me. Two weeks later I realized I had a rib out in my spine. That was what was giving me all the pain. They were giving me painkillers, but I could not figure out why there was a knife in my back."

While he wasn't at the end of his career yet, the two years of injury gave him a glimpse of what it would be like. "When you're injured to the point where you can't do the things that you usually do, I think that's when I'll quit," he explains. "When I say, 'I can't move, I can't do this thing.' When you can't be yourself, the second you feel that, have the guts to call it.

"Retirement will cross my mind, and it won't take long to germinate. I think it will be one day when you do something and you say, 'I used to be able to do that.' And I'm not

Even as a Chief, Super Joe was still schoolin' Young.

gonna say, 'That's okay. I'm smarter now.' I really want to be able to play the game the way I've always been able to play it."

Asked to define that style of his, Young doesn't hesitate. "Recklessly at some level with the ability to get out and move and throw the ball," he says.

RECKLESSLY?

Young's crashing, hardnosed style has led his teammates to say that he's a "quarterback with a linebacker's mentality." Maybe it would be more accurate to describe him as a strong safety. In fact, that's the position he was slated to play in college at Brigham Young University.

The great-great-great grandson of Brigham Young, he grew up in Greenwich, Connecticut, the eldest of Grit and Sherry Young's five children. Grit Young himself had played fullback at BYU in the 1950s, and Steve inherited the old man's athletic ability, as well as the substance of his nickname, "grit."

At age 2, Steve could do pushups and by 3 he could dribble a basketball. By his senior year at Greenwich High, he was an excellent student and captain of the football, basketball and baseball teams. And he lived up to his All-America image—while his friends chugged beers, Young guzzled milk.

Photo by Jim Turner

Because his team ran the option in high school, only colleges with option-oriented offenses recruited him. Still, a Mormon friend encouraged BYU coach LaVell Edwards to offer him a scholarship. But the Utah school was loaded with quarterbacks, and by his sophomore year Young was slated to play in the defensive backfield.

Then the team's new offensive coordinator happened to see him throwing the ball with friends one February afternoon. The coordinator was impressed enough to change the course of Young's career.

Before long, Young found himself charged with the responsibility of replacing BYU legend Jim McMahon at quarterback. It seems that would become the dominant theme of his career. "It was a hard go for me to follow Jim because I was expected to win by 70 and set records," Young explained. "I never had the luxury of learning, or letting an offense jell. That's probably why I started running all over the field like a madman, doing anything I possibly could to win the game. People said I was a quarterback with a linebacker's mentality. I was just a quarterback under tremendous pressure to win."

He answered the call so well for BYU that the LA Express of the upstart United States Football League offered him a $40-million contract in 1984, unprecedented for the time. Although he was slated as the NFL's top pick, Young's father directed him to take the USFL's big money, a move both would regret later. As a rookie, he became the first player in pro football history to pass for 300 yards and rush for 100 in the same game.

But with the demise of the USFL, Young found himself with the Tampa Bay Buccaneers for two unfulfilling seasons until Walsh rescued him in April 1987. Young's appearance in a 49er uniform set up an immediate conflict with Montana that lasted until Super Joe moved on to Kansas City in 1993.

"There's a relationship between the fans and Joe almost like a marriage," said 49ers center Jesse Sapolu. "They were in love with him and didn't want to let go. Steve was like the other woman, and the fans were not willing to accept the divorce. They were very, very stubborn and unfair to Steve, and Steve was a class act."

Indeed, he remained so even after the trade. When Montana led the Chiefs to a victory

The lefty look.

over the 49ers in his first season in Kansas City, Young accepted the fact gracefully. "I learned from the master, and today, the master had a little more to teach the student," Young told reporters afterward.

That opportunity has certainly benefitted Young, Walsh says. "Learning from Joe and watching Joe and . . . being on a team and not having to play immediately."

Yet those lessons didn't save Young from the troubles of adjustment once he stepped in as the starter. He was criticized for making receivers slow down to find his passes. Super Joe's timing was always perfect, right? And then there was Young's annoying habit of running and scrambling every place. Super Joe was never so frenetic. Jerry Rice, the 'Niners' great receiver, was one of the harshest early critics, yet over time he has been converted to one of Young's closest friends. "Steve has nothing to prove now," Rice said defiantly after Young's brilliant Super Bowl performance.

Young's response in good times or bad has been the same basic approach. Live simply and humbly. Although he does make you wonder if he is pretending about his lack of pretension. His basic wardrobe despite his $5.5 million annual salary is T-shirts and jeans. He drove the family's old Oldsmobile until it conked out a few seasons ago at 260,000 miles. For years, his off hours were spent studying for his law degree (which he completed) and peforming a hearty schedule of charity and church work. Plus, he still chugs milk instead of beers.

"He's just the kind of guy you'd want your daughter to marry," says 49ers president Carmen Policy, an assessment dating back to Young's high school days.

He may not have the godlike worship bestowed upon Montana—and he'll likely never get that—but he does have respect, a respect that has been burnished by the pressure. "It's been hard-earned because when you think about it, I was given nothing here," Young says. "I really believe that every bit of respect I've gotten, none of it was free. None of it came by way of just someone liking you. Every bit of it had to be earned. Maybe in some ways, in my own perception, over-earned, like you had to go through extra.

"I knew that coming in. That's not something I wasn't aware of or had a problem with one bit. I understood it all the way. It was frustrating at times, but certainly the respect I feel has been earned."

Unfortunately, the upcoming season will require that he begin the process all over again. For years, the San Francisco offense has ranked at the top of the league, but last season it dipped to sixth overall, its lowest ranking since 1981. There was even a time during the past season when team management pondered the idea of building the offense around another quarterback. But during the offseason, the team allowed its QB of the future, Elvis Grbac, to leave for Kansas City as a free agent.

"Steve Young is our guy," 49ers president Carmen Policy said. "He's the leader of the team. He's done it all for us. We have to respect that. Our confidence is restored. He's reaffirmed that he still has it, and will have it in 1997."

Hearing that is fine, but Young knows he has to step onto the field and prove it. "We've got to reclaim a couple of things we haven't had to reclaim for a lot of years," he says, "and one of them is being the classiest team in the league. I think that carried with it a certain air that helped us win. I think we've lost a little bit of that lustre. And that's not just how you look on the field, it's really how you play. There's a certain style to how you play, and we need to make sure we get that back. We can do that. As long as Jerry Rice is breathing and playing, we can do that."

As he speaks, his voice rings with confidence, and this time there seems to be no pretending, because with Steve Young, when it comes to matters of football, he doesn't have to pause to gain a sense of what is right. Part of that, of course, is the extra weight he's carried, that knowledge that when you dare to follow the great ones and succeed, it's always Monkey Time.

Young can run.

Chapter 6/The Content Of Their Character

Blake makes the Bengal offense a deep proposition.

Jeff Blake is a shade over six feet and weighs 202 pounds. He has a strong arm and a quick release that propelled lightly regarded East Carolina to an 11-1 record in 1991 and a Peach Bowl victory over North Carolina State.

One other thing. He's black.

And that, Blake believes, factored strongly into the stagnant beginning of his pro career. Selected by the New York Jets in the sixth round of the 1992 draft, he did little more than wait around two seasons in New York (he played briefly in three games as a rookie, then spent the rest of his tenure on the inactive list). Former Jets coach Bruce Coslet even admits that his staff overlooked Blake in their attempt to develop bonus baby Browning Nagle.

Perhaps if Coslet had paid a little closer attention to Blake they both might have kept their jobs with the Jets. As it was, Coslet was fired, and the Jets released Blake during the 1994 preseason after opting to keep rookie Glenn Foley out of Boston College.

The move left Blake with what he considered to be further proof that the NFL is racist in its attitudes about what constitutes a good quarterback. "The NFL will go to small schools and get white quarterbacks but won't take blacks from small schools," Blake said shortly before being released. "It's a fact. I'm not complaining. I'm saying give everybody a chance, not just a certain type of people."

Fortunately, Blake was picked up by the Cincinnati Bengals before the '94 season, ironic in that the Bengal offensive coordinator was the same Bruce Coslet who had overlooked him in New York. But the Bengals needed somebody in a hurry, somebody who understood their offensive schemes. Having done his understudy work with the Jets, Blake was eminently qualified. So the Bengals offered him a job as their third-string quarterback, making what amounts to the NFL's version of minimum wage. He gladly accepted.

His "big chance" finally came that October of 1994 after Bengals starter David Klingler and backup Donald Hollas were injured. Some big chance. The Bengal offensive line was in shambles, the running game a joke, and Blake was called in to start against the defending Super Bowl champion Dallas Cowboys and their nasty defense. It mostly seemed like a good opportunity to get his head shoved into his neck.

Jeff, though, was Cool Hand Blake. He responded by taking the Cowboys deep. In the first quarter, he zipped a 67-yard strike to Darnay Scott for a 7-0 lead. Early in the second quarter, he did it again, this time for 55 yards. Like that, he had pumped some life into the winless Bengals. Too bad he couldn't play defense, too. He pushed Cincinnati to the edge before losing narrowly, 23-20.

Revived, the Bengals won two of their next three games with Blake running the show, and the NFL's newest star had been born. In playing experience, however, Blake remained very much a rookie and his performances over the final weeks of the season reflected the usual inconsistency, not to mention a plethora of Bengal problems over which he had no control.

Yet there was little question that Blake had established his leadership, arm strength, mobility, savvy and smarts, which in turn brought more playing time and the opportunity to keep improving.

For fans in Cincinnati, thoroughly doused by disappointment over a run of misery-laden seasons, his emergence was very big news. Their elation grew the next season, when Blake took advantage of his first opportunity as a full-time starter to throw for 3,822 yards and 28 touchdowns, numbers that earned him a trip to the Pro Bowl.

It was obvious that he sometimes struggled with his accuracy while throwing to shorter routes underneath zone coverage. But Blake proved to be a master at scrambling to create, particularly when it came to turning his strong arm loose for deep patterns to the Bengals' corps of tall, athletic receivers, led by Carl Pickens, who could rise up to take the ball away from shorter defensive backs. (The Blake-to-Pickens combo helped Pickens to lead the AFC in receiving in 1996 with 100 receptions and a dozen TDs, many of which were crowd-goosing bombs.)

Blake, like many other quarterbacks, is the son of a coach and has the mindset to succeed. What's more, he's tough and doesn't miss games with injuries (his 41 consecutive starts heading into the 1997 season are second in the league behind Brett Favre), and he does all the extra work that winning requires. Before the '95 season, he even held his own mini-camp with Pickens and Darnay Scott to work on the passing game. Each of the past two seasons, he has continued that camp and pulled even more players into it. When a teammate seems reluctant to attend, Blake merely turns marshalling chores over to his wife, Lewanna, who gets on the phone and lassoes reluctant players into coming. For that reason, the Bengals refer to these sessions as Camp Lewanna.

"He works extremely hard and keeps himself in great shape," Bengals assistant Ken Anderson said of Blake. "He makes everyone else better, and that's what you look for. He inspires confidence in his teammates."

The team, however, continued to struggle under coach David Shula. When the Bengals got off to a 1-6 start in 1996, team management replaced Shula with Coslet, who coaxed them to a 7-2 finish. Blake, meanwhile, turned in another consistently solid season, completing 56 percent of his 549 passing attempts for 3,624 yards, 24 TDs (against 14 INTs) and an 80.3 passing rating. He also rushed for 317 yards and two TDs, his second consecutive season of rushing for better than 300 yards, much of it while racing for his life as the Bengal offensive line broke down time and again in the face of opposing rushes.

But it was after Coslet took over that Blake showed what he could really do. In the season's final five games, he racked up a 104.2 quarterback rating with 13 touchdowns against three interceptions. The result was that the once-puny Bengals scored 372 points, fifth best in the league.

As backup insurance for this season, the team's powers that be have brought back Boomer Esiason, who himself threw for 2,293 yards last season in an up-and-down run in Phoenix that included a couple of monster games in the 400-yards passing range.

Some observers have wondered about the move because Esiason has a biting sense of humor and a penchant for sometimes directing it at teammates. A four-time Pro Bowler, the 36-year-old Esiason still holds the Bengals' single-season passing record (3,959 passing yards in 1986). He has twice led the AFC in passing yards (1987 and 1989) and was named the league's MVP when he led Cincinnati to the Super Bowl following the 1988 season. He also quarterbacked the Bengals to the AFC Central title in 1990. But the team opened to an 0-8 start in 1991, setting the stage for Esiason to be replaced by Dave Klingler in 1992. Cincinnati traded him to the Jets in 1993, where he played for three seasons before heading to the Cardinals for a season. Now Boomer's back, and many observers are wondering if he'll be willing to work as Blake's backup.

"I can't tell you it's the easiest thing to come to grips with," Esiason admitted in training camp. "Nobody wants to be a backup quarterback. But we have a bright, young star at quarterback, and he deserves all that he's been receiving."

Oh yes, this team clearly belongs to Blake. And no one can tell him he hasn't earned it. A fair shot to run the show was all he ever asked for.

MOON MISSION

You don't have to tell Warren Moon about the extra lengths a black quarterback has to go to prove he can play. The troubles began right out of high school in Los Angeles, where he earned All-America honors. The major colleges weren't all that interested, so he played his freshman season at West Los Angeles Junior College and turned in the kind of performances that prompted the University of Washington to offer a scholarship.

He became the Huskies' starting quarterback as a sophomore that next season, a move that wasn't entirely popular with the school's fans. His girlfriend Felicia, who would later become his wife, had to sit in the stands week after week listening to the boos and racially tinged commentary around her.

"It was difficult for me because I was only 18 years old," Moon later recalled. "And it was the first time I had been away from home. There were a couple of times that I thought about giving up, but my mother told me that I had never quit anything before. So I followed her suggestions to stay there, stick it out and make the best of it. But those experiences taught me an awful lot about people."

Moon struggled that season, didn't throw the ball well and wound up starting just six games before moving to part-time duty. The next year, however, he showed a new maturity and held onto the starting job, which mostly involved handing off the ball to the running backs in the Huskies' ground game. He did throw for better than 1,000 yards, presaging the big year he was set to have as a senior.

For 1977, the 6-3, 208-pound Moon passed for better than 1,500 yards and 11 TD passes, which drove the Huskies to a 10-2 record, the PAC-8 championship and a Rose Bowl victory, all of which netted Moon honors as the conference player of the year. He closed out his college career by earning Rose Bowl MVP distinction for pushing Washington to a 27-20 upset of Michigan on New Year's Day 1978.

After the season, there were indications that NFL scouts figured he might be worth a fourth-round pick that spring, but, sensing negative vibes, Moon decided to sign with the Edmonton Eskimos of the Canadian Football League, which proved to be a prudent move because no NFL team bothered to draft him. Over each of the next five years, he shared an increasingly larger load as Edmonton powered its way to five straight Grey Cup championships. In that time he racked up nearly 20,000 passing yards, including two seasons better than 5,000 yards passing, making him the only pro quarterback to break that barrier in a season.

The mega-numbers meant that by 1984 a host of NFL teams were interested in signing him, but Moon turned them all down to follow Edmonton coach Hugh Campbell to the Houston Oilers. Although there had been no black starting quarterbacks in the NFL in 1983, he made the move after talking with James Harris and Doug Williams, both black quarterbacks who had distinguished themselves in the league. They both said it was time for Moon to force the issue.

Moon ran the drill in Houston for a decade.

Moon knew it wouldn't be easy. Once again, the spectre of his mother, Pat, loomed over his decision. The only boy in a family of seven children, Moon was 7 when he lost his father to liver disease. His relationship with his mother, a nurse, was special.

"The biggest thing my mom always tried to tell me was that I could accomplish anything I wanted to in life if I was willing to do what it takes to be successful," he said during a break between photo sessions at the Quarterback Challenge. "She instilled that at a very young age, and it kinda stuck with me. Even though I've been through a lot of tough times in my life and my career, I've always been able to overcome it because of those words and the confidence I've had in myself because of those words."

Moon's strong arm and athletic style were a perfect pairing with the run-and-shoot offense in Houston. The team was generally weak when he arrived in town, but his performances over the next several seasons helped elevate the Oilers to a consistent playoff contender. However, a championship eluded them in a variety of painful ways, including the brutal 1992 fold against Buffalo in which Moon had driven his club to a 28-3 lead over the Bills only to see them mount the greatest comeback in NFL history. Moon sat numbly in the locker room in the aftermath of that debacle and asked, "What happened out there?"

After his tenure in Houston, he moved to the Minnesota Vikings and directed that club to three playoff appearances in three seasons. Now, closing in on his 41st birthday, Moon has signed with the Seattle Seahawks as a backup to John Friez, meaning that he will return to Washington, a move he calls "good karma."

By far his greatest success is the mountain of statistics he has amassed, including 67,885 passing yards, 5,142 completions and 398 touchdown passes over 19 CFL and NFL seasons. Between 1988 and 1995, Moon was named to eight consecutive Pro Bowls. In 1995, at age 39, he threw for 33 touchdowns and completed 62.2 of his passes for the Vikings.

Asked about his prospects for the Hall of Fame, Moon chooses his words cautiously. "It's really hard to say, and I don't know what the criteria is," he says, "but if you look at my numbers, there is no question I should be there. I haven't won an NFL championship, but my teams have been in the playoffs nine consecutive years."

He has come to Seattle with the full understanding that he is a backup. But his arm remains strong and so does his will. "The big thing with me is that I still have the desire," he says.

That becomes apparent as his voice picks up when he's asked about Seattle's impressive corps of pass catchers. "They've got some talented receivers there," Moon says. "I'm really excited about Joey Galloway. I think they need to get the ball in his hands more, and hopefully they will. They're moving his position from the X receiver to the Z receiver, which is more of a main receiver. He needs to have the ball in his hands because he's so good after the catch. Brian Blades has been a proven receiver over the years, very consistent. Mike Pritchard is another guy who's a big-play type guy."

Just as important, he knows the big plays aren't all on the field. His Crescent Moon Foundation raises money each year to fund college scholarships for high school students in Houston. He has also given $500,000 to build a community center for his church.

However, those good deeds couldn't alleviate his humiliation a few years ago when he made headlines after being charged with spousal abuse. He and wife Felicia held their marriage together through the incident, and Moon was later acquitted of criminal charges, although he acknowledged his shortcomings and underwent counseling. "That was a tough time," he says now. "I've never been involved with anything legally or criminally. I had to deal with tough times in football, and my wife and my kids have tough skin. I think that's one of the reasons we were able to make it through this situation."

Asked why fans idolize athletes so much, despite their obvious human failings, Moon said, "I think television and the media have something to do with it, the type of scale they put us on. We're blown up so big nowadays, more than ever before... .

"People forget sometimes that we're still human, that we have some qualities that other people might not have. But other people have qualities that we might not have. We're just gifted in this way. But we're still human when it comes right down to the nuts and bolts of it. People tend to forget that just because we do our craft very well. They think that that translates into the rest of your life as well, that everything else is supposed to be perfect and great and well. But that's not always the case. We're humans, with feelings and problems and concerns and all the things that all other people have."

He does take pride in the fact that his presence and that of other black quarterbacks over the years has made it easier for African Americans to be accepted in the position today.

"I think the quarterback position has changed a little bit," he says. "I think there's more opportunity for young black quarterbacks. But the coaching situation as far as African Americans becoming head coaches took a giant step backwards in the fact that there were 10 jobs open (in 1996-97) and only one African American interviewed for a job. I think there's a lot more qualified coaches out there. They're not asking to be given the job; they just want the opportunity to go in there and interview like everybody else."

His main satisfaction, one that seems tangible to his many fans, is that he has established a level of competence that supercedes any question of race. "People can't label me any type of quarterback," he says. "I've done a lot of different things and had a lot of success in a lot of different things."

SLASH

Slash, that's Kordell Stewart's nickname, and he's earned it. But the circumstances behind it are about to change. In his two seasons with the Pittsburgh Steelers, Stewart's position has been listed as quarterback/receiver/running back. In other words, he's that player with the rare athletic ability to play all those positions, requiring slashes between the designations.

Kordell was the slash man in Pittsburgh.

Now, however, Slash is scheduled to become simply a quarterback. It's a position change Stewart has longed for, but he's made scant little noise about the issue over the past two seasons because he's clearly the type of guy who puts the team first.

Now, however, Stewart's and the team's interests have merged. In his third NFL season, Stewart has become the Steelers' best option as a starting quarterback.

Rick Neuheisel, Stewart's coach at the University of Colorado, had seen this day coming.

"Kordell can flourish as anything," Neuheisel said in 1995, "but it would be a tragedy if he wasn't given the opportunity at quarterback. There isn't a throw he can't make, as long as he knows exactly what he's looking at. He can be phenomenal.

"Factor in how defenses are going to be absolutely scared of his ability to run, and then you take away man coverage. If they play man, and he breaks through the line of scrimmage, everyone will have their backs to him and he will not only run for a first down, but he will score a touchdown. I guarantee you that Steve Bono's record 76-yard run for a touchdown by a quarterback will be broken. Kordell will go farther."

Indeed, Stewart broke the record in 1996, ripping off an 80-yard run as an occasional QB. Neuheisel had no trouble making the prediction after watching Stewart's college work for the Buffaloes, particularly his famous last-second pass to receiver Michael Westbrook that defeated Michigan in 1994.

"He had fumbled with five minutes left in the game, and we were down 26-14," Neuheisel recalled. "But instead of going over and withdrawing, he said, 'I'm sorry, fellas. We are going to get back.' People believed him, and everyone knows how that game ended."

Stewart has been inspiring that kind of confidence in teammates since his earliest involvement with the game. In middle school he played running back, but when he moved to high school as a freshman he switched positions.

"I had a baseball and a little football and threw them one day in practice at middle school," Stewart recalled. "Guys in middle school saw how far I could throw. The same guys I played ball with there wound up going to high school with me. One day the coach said, 'We need a quarterback,' and everybody said, 'Kordell can play quarterback!' I was like, 'Huh-uh.' "

Reluctant as he was, the new position was a natural, Stewart said. "Ever since then, I've been doing it. I was an option quarterback then, but I didn't turn into a passing quarterback until my sophomore year in college.'"

His admiration of Bears great Walter Payton is something that dates to his earliest days in the game. "I was a running back when I was small," Stewart said of Payton. "He was one of those guys I admired. Still to this day he is. . . . I didn't know that much about him, but just his style. The way he played was hard, aggressive. Regardless of what happened, he wanted to win. That's what I like to do."

Stewart's competitiveness drove Colorado to an 11-1 record in 1994 and helped make him a second-round pick of the Steelers in the '95 draft. He was the fourth quarterback in

Making the reads is big for Kordell.

their camp that summer behind starter Neil O'Donnell, backup Mike Tomzak and third-stringer Jim Miller. But the coaches were aware of his athleticism as a runner. After injuries left the team thin at wide receiver, the coaches asked if he would mind working there some.

Whatever helps the team, Stewart told them.

Immediately the coaches saw that he gave the Steelers' excellent defensive backfield fits in practice. Nobody could cover him.

When the Steelers started with three wins and four losses that fall of '95, the coaches decided to use Stewart more to help the team score. A young black man intent on being a quarterback could have been offended by the circumstances. "I see it from a positive side," Stewart said at the time, "because it's something where I have the ability. And it was an opportunity to help the team. If I was the fourth quarterback, I wouldn't have been dressing."

Stewart's play was just the spark the Steelers needed to start on a run that carried them all the way to the Super Bowl. Like that, he evolved into Slash, an unusual offensive force playing three positions in the NFL. At first, he was the team's fifth wide receiver. Then the coaches began using his multiple skills to run gadget plays that helped confuse defenses into giving up big gains. On Monday Night Football, he threw a touchdown pass in a win over Cleveland. Then he pulled in a 71-yard scoring pass to help drive a come-from-behind victory over the Bengals. Against New England, he ran for a score. The versatility thrilled Pittsburgh fans, his teammates and the coaches. His offensive potential brought an excitement, an electricty, that charged the season.

"The way I played my rookie year, I think guys enjoyed it," Stewart says now, during a break at the Quarterback Challenge. "And I did, too. We all jelled together as a team."

All the while, Stewart badly wanted to play quarterback, but he didn't let those feelings get in the way. At the same time, he became more determined than ever in his plans to reach that goal. "I'm just a person who wants to win," he explained. "I hate losing. For me to get out there and play the receiver position and the running back position as well as I did, that was because I felt that was a challenge to me and I needed to get it accomplished."

The Steelers lost to the Dallas Cowboys in the Super Bowl, but Stewart's megawatt future had been established. Then, abruptly, O'Donnell left via free agency for a giant contract with the New York Jets, and suddenly the starting quarterback job was open. Tomzak, Miller and Stewart battled for it in training camp, and the coaches awarded the job to Miller. Then after one game, they switched to Tomzak.

"Just accepting the fact that I wasn't going to start as a quarterback was my biggest challenge," Stewart says now. "That's mental, physical, whatever you want to call it."

Tomzak ran the show for 1996. The numbers tell the story: Tomzak completed 55 percent of his 401 passing attempts for 2,767 yards. He had 15 TDs and 17 interceptions. Stewart, as backup, completed only 37 percent of his 30 attempts, but he also rushed for five scores and rang up three TDs and another 293 yards as a receiver.

Will he throw or go?

Together, the two quarterbacks helped drive Pittsburgh to the playoffs for the fifth straight season. Unfortunately, their efforts ended in a dismal outing against New England. Unable to get something going offensively, the coaches turned to Stewart. But a quarterback needs more than occasional work to produce in the clutch. Stewart failed to complete any of his 10 passes that day.

The performance stung Stewart, but in the aftermath coach Bill Cowher's staff assured him that he would get a chance to start this season. It was clear that developing his talent would certainly be in the interest of this club. Where Tomzak is merely functional, Stewart has weapon potential.

"That's my intention," Stewart said when asked about starting. "For coach Cowher to make that decision, that's up to him. But that's the way my frame of mind is. I feel it's wide open and time to take advantage.

"I've been blessed with so much talent," he added. "I don't take it for granted, but there's not much as far as the physical aspect is concerned that I don't think I can't do, besides playing noseguard and that good stuff. But as far as the build and strength and ability to be fast and run, I have it. I just need to keep in mind that it came from up above and not myself. I just need to take everything a step at a time."

Stewart said that he didn't see any racism involved in the decision to use him as a Slash his first two seasons. "It's a great opportunity because all the things I've done in the past have done nothing but help me up until this point," he explained. "People are like, 'He's a great receiver; he can run the ball. He can do this; he can do that.' If I had been just a quarterback sitting on the bench, having the opportunity to start this year would be much harder basically because I wouldn't have had the opportunity to get out there and be amongst all the hoopla and excitement and stuff like that. But now that I've been out there, hopefully my chance will come, given to me by the coaches. The understanding and knowing and feeling what's going to happen will be there. It's just a matter of getting out there and relaxing and letting the game come to be, just being poised and having fun."

He looks at playing quarterback as the most special of athletic challenges. "That's where all the pressure comes in and all the stereotypical things that go along with it," he said. "It's a matter of how I handle it. I just need to relax basically, just let the game come to me. I know I can do it. Just let things develop."

In a large part his confidence is imbedded in a strong sense of personal style. "I'm a guy who don't say too much on the field," he says, "but I think my reaction shows that I want to win and I want to get things accomplished. I think guys feed off that. You can say, 'Guys, let's go!' Then you get out there and make a mistake and all of a sudden you're like, 'Damn, I can't say too much.' So my best thing is just to react. And that's all I can do, is just react."

As Stewart had hoped, Cowher named him the starting quarterback heading into camp, a promotion for which Stewart rewarded his coach by leading the Steelers to a 30-17 exhibition win over the Bears in the first NFL game ever played in Ireland in late July.

Typical of most exhibitions, Stewart only played a quarter, but he started the game with three straight completions and wound up hitting seven of 11 passes for 131 yards, which put the Steelers ahead, 10-0. "I think Kordell did a great job," Cowher said. "He was able to see the field, he kept his poise and obviously threw the ball very accurately."

"It was a great experience to get out there and actually run some things with the first team," Stewart said.

The Steelers had come into the season thinking that their primary offensive function would be built around big back Jerome Bettis, but after watching Stewart's work, the coaches were contemplating a four-receiver set that would keep the field wide open for both Bettis and Stewart.

"Kordell has such a strong arm, it gives us a lot of options," Cowher said happily. "It opens it up for those receivers."

"I just need to practice at the quarterback position because I have raw athletic ability," Stewart had told me at the Quarterback Challenge. "But to actually take all that ability and turn it into a fine quarterback…"

The thought of that put a gleam in his eye and led him to talk of how he envisions his house when he gets one not too far down the road. He wants a special room, with toys, games, a TV, and a lineup of all the helmets in the league. They'll all be mini-helmets, except for his Steelers headgear.

"Have my big helmet," he says laughing, "but have mini-helmets for all the rest of them, indicating that my team is the dominant team."

It's a fitting vision for a man who will do whatever it takes to make his team a winner. It leads you to suspect that the slash in his name is only just beginning. Down the road, the job description could well include quarterback/Super Bowl champion/MVP.

Chapter 7/Shifting With Spectral Swiftness

t grew out of gross behavior, this matter of being a running back. You see, football evolved from English soccer way back in the 19th century, and back then the Brits were eternally annoyed with Americans because they kept picking up the damn ball and running with it, which was a no-no.

"Don't you Yanks have the common decency to obey the rules?" the Brits used to say.

"Yes," the Americans would reply, "we understand the rules. But running with the ball is so natural. Why don't you just pick that sucker up and head for the goal?"

We've come a long way since those first glimmering days of American football. Now we have high-tech offenses and strong-armed quarterbacks to fling the ball 80 yards upfield. But the essence of the sport remains the running game, the ability of a very special back to take the pigskin and sprint, cut, glide, shift, shag his way upfield for a gain. That has been, and always will be, the safest, simplest way to advance the ball.

Faced with that basic assignment, it didn't take the game's early coaches long to discover the prototype for a great runner. Strong, swift, shifty, durable, someone able to run over or around the opposition.

It was Jim Thorpe's good fortune to possess all of those characteristics and come along just as early rules changes, including the forward pass, had opened up the game from its early "three yards and a cloud of dust" approach. Because of that, we think of him as the first great running back.

A two-time All-American at Carlisle Indian School in Pennsylvania, Thorpe went on to a long, distinguished pro career. He had the speed and shiftiness to get around tacklers, but he also had the size and strength to run over them, which is what he preferred to do, because of his great competitive nature. He so loved to smash a tackler, in fact, that toward the end of his career, as his prowess waned, he was accused of fashioning a pair of hard leather shoulder pads and lacing them with metal rivets, just so he could still deliver that special pop to defenders.

The next great link in the evolutionary chain of the ball carrier, Red Grange, "the Galloping Ghost," emerged at the University of Illinois in the 1920s. While the pro game was struggling to gather a fan following, Big Ten college football was regularly pulling in 80,000 spectators in that first great Golden Age of sport, and Grange, also known as the

Eric D. had the skillz to go upfield, uknowhatI'msayin'?

"Wheaton Iceman," was the primary attraction. It was also the age of the great sportswriters, and Grantland Rice composed prose poems for newspaper leads lionizing Grange's graceful, deceptive style:

"There are two shapes now moving,

Two ghosts that drift and glide,

And which of them to tackle,

Each rival must decide;

They shift with spectral swiftness,

Across the swarded range,

And one of them's a shadow,

And one of them is Grange."

This, in fact, stirred up such a media frenzy that the Chicago Bears signed Grange as soon as he completed his last game at Illinois in the late fall of 1925, just in time for him to join the team at Thanksgiving. The press claimed the move was a crass show of professionalism, but Grange brought his fan following to the struggling NFL. Many franchises were fighting for survival until the Bears launched a season-ending Grange exhibition tour that filled every stadium they visited. The exhibition was so successful, they launched a second tour in Miami on Christmas day that saw Grange play 19 games in 17 cities in just over 66 days.

The pace left him exhausted and injured, and in fact, his career would be shortened by injuries, but there was no question that Grange was the running back who popularized pro football and headed it toward financial prosperity.

The next early prototype, the big, swift back, also wore a Bears uniform. Bronko Nagurski, a 6-foot-2, 225-pounder, was a dominant ball carrier during the early 1930s. There are many legends about his size, strength and toughness, but perhaps the most indicative was the story that he once collided with a policeman's horse standing on the sidelines and knocked the poor animal out cold. When you consider that Bronk was wearing only a leather helmet, that's quite a bash.

Such feats presaged the emergence of the NFL after World War II and the arrival of the kinds of backs who could thrill crowds with their ability to "break one." There was a special magic about a ball carrier's slashing through the line of scrimmage and into the open field that could force a collective gasp from spectators. It's the same kind of thrill that follows the special crack of the bat at the launching of a home run, or the grunt of the rim on a monster slam dunk.

Yet, in another sense, those are lesser feats, because the ball carrier faces a much more severe physical challenge in a climate that is far more threatening. Each line buck, each cut against the grain, offers the potential for major injury. That helps explain why the constant battering reduces the average running back's career to only four seasons.

That's all the more reason to honor the special talents and durability of the men who work the most dangerous landscape. Some had fancy gliding styles. Others used bull power. Some were slashers.

The following top the list of the best:

• Jim Brown. Probably the toughest competitor in the history of the game. An All-American in both football and lacrosse at Syracuse University, the 6-2, 238-pound Brown was the NFL's rookie of the year in 1957. An eight-time All-Pro, he led the league in rushing every year except one during his nine-year career and was voted player of the year in 1958, 1963 and 1965.

He retired in 1966 at the age of 30, but by then he had already amassed 12,312 yards rushing on 2,359 carries. He scored 106 rushing touchdowns and another 20 receiving.

• Emmitt Smith. You've maybe heard of this guy. The centerpiece in a Dallas Cowboys' offense that has won four Super Bowls, the 5-9, 209-pound Smith has rushed for 10,160 yards in just seven seasons and scored 115 touchdowns. Now, at age 28, his biggest challenge may be the offseason conditioning work necessary to have the longevity to challenge Walter Payton's all-time rushing yardage record.

• Walter Payton. The game's all-time rushing yardage leader with 16,726 yards, the 5-10, 203-pound Payton came out of Jackson State in 1975 to join the Bears. Over his 13-year career, he rushed for more than 1,000 yards in 10 seasons and scored 110 touchdowns. A fine blocker and receiver, the superbly conditioned Payton was the league's player of the year in 1985. His nickname, "Sweetness," belied just how tough he was.

• Tony Dorsett. In many regards, he was the Lamborghini of running backs, with a sleek style, great vision and speed aplenty. A two-time All-American at the University of Pittsburgh, Dorsett claimed the 1976 Heisman, then followed it up with 1977 NFL rookie of the year honors as a Dallas Cowboy. In each of his first six pro seasons, Touchdown Tony rang up more than 1,000 yards on the ground and concluded his playing days with the Denver Broncos in 1988 with a career total of 12,379,yards.

• Barry Sanders. This guy is Fred Astaire in cleats. He won the Heisman as a junior at Oklahoma State in 1988, then hopped to the Detroit Lions, where in eight seasons the 5-8, 203 pounder has rushed for 11,725 yards and scored 91 touchdowns while averaging a super 4.9 yards per carry (Sanders also has another 2,180 yards and seven touchdowns receiving). If you've spent any Sunday afternoons on the couch watching the tube, you know about his dance steps on the carpet at the Pontiac Silverdome.

- Eric Dickerson. At 6-3, 230 pounds, this guy had rare size and speed. He came out of Southern Methodist to earn rookie of the year honors with the Los Angeles Rams in 1982 and was named NFC player of the year the next season with a league-leading 1,808 yards rushing . He rushed for more than 1,000 yards in seven consecutive seasons, a record. In 1984, he also set the league's single-season rushing mark with 2,105 yards. He again led the league in rushing as a Ram in 1986, then moved on to the Indianapolis Colts and again led the league in '88. For all of his grand totals, however, his career was marked by clashes with coaches and management. A five-time All-Pro, he retired in 1993, with better than 13,000 career yards, second on the all-time list.

- O.J. Simpson. Forget the white Bronco for a moment and look at just his football career. The 6-1, 212-pound Simpson won the Heisman Trophy at Southern Cal in 1969, then moved on to the Buffalo Bills, where he was a part-time player until moving into the starting lineup in 1972 and becoming a star. In 1973, he became the first back to rush for more than 2,000 yards in a season. He finished his career with the 49ers in 1979 and amassed career totals of 11,236 yards and 76 touchdowns. He was acquitted of the murder of his wife and a male friend in 1995.

- Franco Harris. Nothing fancy here, just power. The 6-2, 225-pound Harris was a blocking fullback at Penn State who found stardom in the NFL. He was a key factor for four Pittsburgh Steeler Super Bowl championship teams and was MVP of Super Bowl IX, when he gained 158 yards on 34 carries. In his 13 years as a pro, he gained 12,120 yards and scored 91 TDs rushing.

- John Riggins. The 6-2, 230-pound Riggo came out of the University of Kansas to the New York Jets in 1971 and jumped to the Washington Redskins in 1976 as a free agent. The big hoss in the Redskins' single-back offense, Riggins was named most valuable player of Super Bowl XVII, after he rushed for 166 yards in 38 attempts to lead Washington over Miami. He was named the league's player of the year in 1983 after rushing for 1,347 yards and a record 24 touchdowns. Over his 14-year career, he rushed for 11,352 yards and 104 touchdowns.

- Earl Campbell. This 5-11, 230-pounder could hammer defenses inside with his power, then turn on his speed to break into the open for long gains. He won the Heisman at the University of Texas in 1977, then moved to the Houston Oilers and led the NFL in rushing for four straight seasons, from 1977 to 1981, until injuries began to limit his playing time. He retired in 1985, having gained 9,407 yards over his career and scored 74 touchdowns.

- Gale Sayers. A brilliant open-field runner out of the University of Kansas, Sayers went to the Chicago Bears and was named rookie of the year in 1965. He led the league in rushing in 1966 and 1969. Knee injuries forced his early retirement in 1971 but not before he had rung up 9,435 career yards and 56 touchdowns.

- Marcus Allen. Although he suffered through several seasons of disuse as a Los Angeles Raider, the 6-2, 210-pound Allen has gained 11,738 yards rushing and scored 134 touchdowns over his 15-year pro career. He has gained better than 5,000 yards as a receiver. At Southern Cal, he set the NCAA single-season rushing record with 2,432 yards.

- Ottis Anderson. He set a rookie rushing record with the St. Louis Cardinals in 1979 (1,605 yards), then followed that with four 1,000-yard seasons over the next five years. He was traded to New York in 1986 and gained 1,023 yards in 1989. In addition, he was named the MVP of Super Bowl XXV with 102 yards rushing in the Giants' 20-19 win over Buffalo.

- Thurman Thomas. This 5-10, 198-pounder out of Oklahoma State has gained 10,762 yards over his first nine NFL seasons. His play was a key factor in the Buffalo Bills reaching four Super Bowls, but critics charge it was also a factor in the Bills losing all four championship games.

- Roger Craig. He was a power player for three San Francisco 49er Super Bowl championship teams. He was the first back in history to gain more than 1,000 yards both rushing and receiving in one season (1985) and owns the single-season record for receptions by a running back with 92.

- Herschel Walker. If you count his yardage in the United States Football League, Walker has gained more rushing real estate than any human being. As it is, his 8,122 yards rushing and 60 touchdowns in 10 NFL seasons ain't bad. Plus he has another 4,621 yards and 19 more touchdowns receiving.

- Jim Taylor. At 215 pounds, this LSU product didn't have the size to play pro fullback, but he was a fixture on Vince Lombardi's Green Bay Packer teams. For three straight seasons— 1960-62—he gained more than 1,000 yards and led the league in rushing in 1962. For his career, he gained 8,597 yards and scored 96 touchdowns.

- Larry Csonka. He built a reputation as a hard runner and dependable blocker while leading the Miami Dolphins to their glory seasons in the early 1970s. He was named the MVP of Super Bowl VIII after gaining 145 yards on 33 carries to power Miami past Minnesota for the championship. A 6-3, 235-pounder, he rushed for 8,081 yards in 11 NFL seasons.

- Steve Van Buren. This five-time All-Pro graduated from LSU in 1943 and went on to power the Philadelphia Eagles to two NFL titles. He led the league in rushing in 1945 and '47, '48 and '49, and gained 195 yards rushing in the Eagles' 1949 championship win over the Rams.

   Eager to push past these great backs in the record books is a host of exciting young runners in the NFL today, including:

- Karim Abdul-Jabbar, a guy who averaged better than five yards per carry his final two seasons at UCLA, then went to the Miami Dolphins as a third-round pick in 1996 and became the surprise of the AFC by rushing for 1,116 yards and 11 touchdowns. "We're going to run the football," coach Jimmy Johnson said after watching Abdul-Jabbar work, something that hadn't been said in Miami in two decades.

- Eddie George, who claimed the Heisman at Ohio State then joined the Houston (now Tennessee) Oilers as a first-round pick in 1996 and promptly set about proving that he was worthy of any award people wanted to give him. He rushed for 1,368 yards, good enough to be named Offensive Rookie of the Year and just 82 yards short of Earl Campbell's rookie rushing record. Judging from his work ethic, there are more prizes waiting in George's future. "I know I have to get even better," he says. "There are a lot of things to improve on — blocking, passing routes, reading blocks."

- Terry Allen, who with eight years experience is an old man by most standards, has overcome reconstructive surgery on both knees to turn in two brilliant seasons for the Washington Redskins. A 5-10, 208-pounder out of Clemson, Allen had been released by Minnesota in 1994 because of his injuries. He signed with Washington and rushed for 1,309 yards and 10 touchdowns in 1995, then followed that up with another 1,353 yards and 21 TDs in '96, all the product of his intense labor. "What Terry means to our team goes a lot further than the yards rushing and the touchdowns," says Washington coach Norv Turner. "It's a day-to-day work ethic."

   "It's something I knew I could do if given the opportunity," Allen said of his big '96 season, which earned him a new $14.8 million, four-year contract. "I feel like I'm one of the best backs in the league."

- Ricky Watters, a guy who has dispensed a lot of headaches in his six seasons of NFL play — to both the management of the teams he has played for as well as his would-be tacklers. His style is nothing pretty, but it is hard-nosed and effective. He has rushed for nearly 6,000 yards, first for San Francisco, then for the Philadelphia Eagles. In 1996, he pushed the Philly offense along with 1,411 yards rushing and 13 TDs and another 444 yards receiving.

• Terrell Davis, who spent much of his senior season injured at the University of Georgia, wasn't drafted until the sixth round of the 1995 draft (the 196th player selected), but he began covering big ground in the Denver Broncos' training camp, moving from eighth on the depth charts into position to eventually take over the starting chores his rookie season. He finished his first year with 1,117 yards rushing, so impressive that his teammates voted him Denver's MVP. For 1996, he pumped his numbers to 1,538 yards rushing, good enough to push him into the Pro Bowl and honors as the Associated Press Offensive Player of the Year. He also finished third in the league MVP voting. All this he accomplished without really aspiring to play pro football, Davis says. "I really didn't play much in high school. I thought that would be the last of my football. Then I went to college and thought that would be the end of it."

Now, with the fast start to his pro career, he's on a track to become one of the all-time greats.

• Curtis Martin, a 5-11, 203-pounder who came out of the University of Pittsburgh in 1995 as a third-round draft pick of the New England Patriots, to earn Rookie of the Year honors and a trip to the Pro Bowl. His credentials? How 'bout 1,487 yards rushing and 14 TDs. Martin followed that up in '96 with another 1,152 yards rushing, a major factor in the Patriots making their way to the Super Bowl. "When I'm running the ball," Martin says, "it's almost like a state of panic or a paranoid state. As soon as I see a hand, I'm jerking away from it. I run to where the defenders are not."

Spoken like a guy who knows the true value of skillz.

Part II It's Skillz That Thrillz

he ancient Greeks played an early version of football and called it harpaston. Typical of their cultural copycat style, the Romans played harpastum. The Italians in the Middle Ages dubbed their game calcio. On the other side of the globe, the Polynesians shredded bamboo to make a ball for kicking, while the Eskimo stuffed moss into a leather hide.

Whatever the culture, whatever the implements, the phenomenon of football has struck a chord of pride, manhood and meanness in young men over the centuries. The game has appealed to the rakishness of their egos, to the baseness of their desire for power and physical prowess.

Its promoters have touted it as a test of toughness and character. Its detractors have decried it as an expression of violence, a glorification of brute force.

Its analysts suggest that while the game feeds on aggression, football has become an effective release valve for modern man, giving him the opportunity to vent the dark side of his nature in a controlled setting.

Perhaps there's some merit to that opinion. As militaristic a genius as Vince Lombardi was, he never ordered his troops to march on Moscow. Yet that line of thinking is a bit too esoteric for football, a wonderfully uncomplicated pastime.

The simple essence of the game is contact. Hitting. Ringing an opponent's bell, so to speak. Ask an 18-year-old linebacker his feelings on the greater issues of the sport, and he'll tell you he just wants to knock somebody's jock off.

Any number of theories have been advanced on the origins of modern football. One of the more interesting traces the American professional game to the Danish invasion and occupation of England between 1016 to 1042.

It seems that a number of Danes were killed and buried on the field of battle, only to be disinterred during ploughing a number of years later, after the English had driven the Danes from their island.

As Danish skulls were turned up by the plough, the farmhands made quite a game of kicking them about the field. It's a gruesome tale, yet it does seem suited to the territorial urge that pervades modern football. The whole game, in fact, is built on protecting one's home goal from invaders.

Kicking games played by crowds of unruly youths were much in evidence in England throughout the ensuing centuries. The object kicked was usually an inflated cow or pig's bladder, usually procured immediately after butchering in late fall. Some enthusiasts went so far as to cover the bladder with leather hide.

The game knew few boundaries, with any landmark serving as a goal. There was no limit to players on a side. In fact, the game of "futballe," as it was called in 12th century England, often drew large crowds, which, once caught up in the movement of the game, were known to wreak havoc on communities, trampling gardens, breaking down fences and creating a general mayhem.

Often the competition raged between villages, pitting the youthful population of one

Photo by Tim Umphrey

Tim Brown has killa skillz, just like Lynn Swann used to display.

locality against another. It is no surprise that authorities considered football a nuisance. Fearing the games would distract the population from the archery practice needed for England's military preparedness, King Henry II, who reigned from 1154 to 1189, banned the sport.

"No more futballe," Henry is said to have declared.

Edward II did the same when he was king from 1307-27, as did Henry VI in the early 15th century.

In 1314, Edward's laws forbade "hustling over large footballs, from which many evils arise, which God forbid." Football, though, was beyond the law.

Like a weed, the game persisted and flourished, wrapping itself like a vine in the English cultural heritage, capturing the fancy of generation after generation of schoolboys and ruffians. By Shakespeare's time, football was described as a "friendlie kind of fyghte... a bloody and murthering practice."

By the 17th century, the town fathers of Manchester railed against "a company of lewd and disordered persons using that unlawful exercise of playing with the football in the streets... breaking many men's windowes and glasse at their pleasure and other great inormyties..."

Considering all of this, it's no wonder that centuries later, playing the American version of the sport, athletes took a special delight in perpetrating smashmouth football, suiting up in pads and helmets with the idea of bashing each other into submission.

In fact, the game might have become nothing more than an exercise in brutality if the athletic skills of the players hadn't evolved as a means of neutralizing the violent landscape. The running game and the forward pass were developed as ways of getting over or around or past the collisions on the line of scrimmage.

It was the skills that opened up the game and thrilled the fans, skills that delivered the heroes from the their three yards and a cloud of dust.

Perhaps the classic of example of the phenomenon of skills was receiver Lynn Swann, a wisp of gentility amidst the Pittsburgh Steelers' brutality.

At least that was his image, an image, of course, that began with his name.

Lynn Swann.

W.B. Yeats couldn't have come up with anything more poetic. The sportswriters immediately reached for descriptions of grace and splendor. Swann surely was all of those things. He could run, he could leap, he could catch, all with a style to match his name.

Yet it was his toughness that brought him the MVP award of Super Bowl X, a toughness that matched his gritty teammates.

The Steelers won four Super Bowls between 1974 and 1980, and to say they did it in "blue-collar" fashion would be more than a bit trite. Yet there's hardly a way around it. In the age of America's great industrial decline, the Steelers were a lingering symbol of potency.

They were hard, polished Pittsburgh steel, running roughshod over the competition with a defense led by Mean Joe Greene, Jack Lambert, L.C. Greenwood, Jack Ham and Mel Blount. The offense had a similar cast with runningbacks Rocky Bleier and Franco Harris and quarterback Terry Bradshaw.

Swann was a mere rookie when the Steelers used their defensive viciousness to subdue the Minnesota Vikings, 16-6, in Super Bowl IX. By the next season, Swann had matured into one of the game's truly gifted pass catchers. Teamed with John Stallworth, he opened up the Steeler offense and helped lead the team to a consecutive Super Bowl appearance.

Along the way, Swann collected his share of bruises, particularly in the AFC title game, a slugfest with the Oakland Raiders. The Steelers won, 16-10, but in the third period Swann collapsed after being nailed by Raider safety George Atkinson. Doctors diagnosed a concussion and kept Swann for observation. Immediately, questions were raised about Swann's ability to play against the Dallas Cowboys in the Super Bowl two weeks away.

Yet within a week, Swann had returned to a limited participation in practice. As it became more apparent he would play in the Super Bowl, the Cowboys began speculating on his effectiveness. Would the head injury make him gun shy?

Swann admitted some doubt. "I thought about it," he told reporters before the game. "But finally I said the heck with it. I'm going out there and playing 100 percent."

Still, all the lingering uncertainty wasn't removed until well into the first quarter at Miami's Orange Bowl. The Cowboys had used quarterback Roger Staubach and their shotgun offense to blast to a 7-0 lead. Then Swann stoked the Steelers' first scoring drive with a leaping, acrobatic catch of a Bradshaw pass at the Dallas 16. Somehow, he had retrieved the ball in midair from sailing incomplete out of bounds, then he twisted to land inbounds. Good for 32 yards, the play set up a scoring pass to tight end Randy Grossman moments later.

The teams traded an odd collection of field goals and a safety thereafter until midway into the final quarter. Holding a 15-10 lead at their own 36, Bradshaw and Swann opted for the bomb. Swann set sail, and Bradshaw lofted a fat one for him to run under. The result was another elegant passage in Swann's highlight poem: a 64-yard gamebuster for a 21-10 lead.

On the downside, Bradshaw was knocked silly by the Dallas rush on the play and lost for the rest of the game.

Staubach brought the Cowboys right back with a quick touchdown pass, then got the ball back again trailing 21-17. But the Steel Curtain defense closed out the Dallas performance by intercepting Staubach's final Hail Mary attempt.

The MVP trophy belonged to Swann, who had caught four passes for 161 yards. Not a bad day's work for a blue collar bird.

He was merely one of the best in a succession of athletes who delivered football's special magic to the fans. Part II of *Smashmouth* is about the game's magicians with skills. The skillz that thrillz.

Chapter 8/Sweet Baby Bus

Photo by Tim Umphrey

Bettis is da Bus in Pitt!

Gladys Bettis, mother of Jerome, the 5-foot-11, 243-pound "Bus" of the Pittsburgh Steelers, likes to tell people that her son got the best of both sides of his lineage.

From his father, Johnnie, an electrical inspector for the city of Detroit, Jerome inherited toughness. Mrs. Bettis doesn't like to say her husband is gruff, but he takes no flack off landlords and builders. "My husband doesn't mess around," she says. "He's a strong man. Jerome got his strength from his dad."

From his mother, Bettis drew his sweetness. As he grew up, she seldom let Jerome, the youngest of her three children, stray too far from her sight. The result of this extra affection is obvious today. His smile is so big, Bettis has to squint just to see over it.

"He's always been very sweet and very gentle," Mrs. Bettis says. "When he was in college at Notre Dame, I would call his dorm and ask where 'my baby' was, or I'd say, 'Where's the baby?' The coaches, all the guys on the team, knew I called him that. He hated it, but he's gotten used to it now."

As you might expect, his reputation on the football field strays a bit from his mother's perspective. Out there, Bettis displays neither his mother's sweetness nor his father's gruff strength. Come game time, the smile disappears and his eyes grow mean and narrow. It's then that Bettis becomes his own man, a bone-crunching ball of competitive fire who takes special delight in punishing the linebackers and defensive backs who get in his way.

Although he's just 25, Bettis has already become a master of the conquerer's code: First you smash opposing defenses, then you talk trash. The physical battering always precedes the psychological warfare.

Smash, then trash.

"He likes to talk to the defensive guys," former teammate Leo Goeas says of Bettis. "He'll tell a defensive back, 'You can't mess with this. You'll have to get up better than that.'"

Today, this style is almost an essential ingredient in the play-action offense. You batter defenses with the running game and taunt the defensive backs into closing in to play the run. Then, if things go according to plan, you burn them with the play-action pass.

It's a simple approach to a simple game, yet the passing has proved the tricky part of the equation for the NFL teams Bettis has played for.

First, there were the downtrodden Los Angeles Rams. For years, they struggled to find a quarterback and an offense. The second quest of the search was seemingly answered in 1993 when Bettis was an unsung rookie.

In that one short pro season, the Rams gained a measure of offense, and Bettis went from a relatively obscure prospect to near superstar status. It all began early that October of 1993 when he had the first of a string of 100-yard rushing games, the capstone of which was a 212-yard afternoon against the New Orleans Saints in December. By the time he was through, Bettis had amassed 1,429 yards rushing, just 58 yards shy of taking the league rushing title from Emmitt Smith. All of this he accomplished while secretly nursing a partially separated shoulder over the last two months of the season.

Although the Rams finished 5-11 and last in the NFC West that year, it was the kind of performance that pumped some new life into the once-proud franchise and reminded many of 1983, when a rookie named Eric Dickerson rushed for 1,808 yards. In fact, only five rookies in pro football history—Dickerson, George Rogers, Ottis Anderson, Barry Sanders and Earl Campbell—have rushed for more yardage.

In the aftermath, Bettis made a trip to the Pro Bowl. And *The Sporting News*, Associated Press, *Pro Football Weekly* and the Pro Football Writers Association all named him the rookie of the year. Plus the trading card industry did something of a backflip over the young power-back. The Rams' public relations staff reported that Bettis was the subject of 80 different trading cards — "More than any rookie in NFL history," the Rams PR office declared (which may say more about the trading card industry than it does about Bettis).

Still, his effort was even more impressive considering that the rest of the Rams' offense was puny and opposing defenses were able to key on him.

What makes his story even better was that Bettis wasn't the back the Rams wanted in the 1993 draft. The team coveted Georgia's Garrison Hearst but couldn't work a trade up to get him. When Hearst went to Phoenix, the Rams settled for Bettis, who had turned pro after playing fullback three seasons for Notre Dame. His college numbers were decent—1,912 yards for a 5.7 average carry over his career—but some observers wondered if Bettis could make the transition from college fullback to pro tailback.

He had sat for a time behind starter Cleveland Gary, but once he got playing time, the progress was dramatic. Suddenly, Bettis was eager to prove that his rookie season was no fluke. "My goal is 2,000 yards this year," he declared before the 1994 season opened, "and if Emmitt is setting his goal anything short of that, then he's going to be a little short when it comes time for someone to win the rushing title. If someone can get 2,100 yards, they're going to lead the league, but if they don't get 2,000, they are going to be behind me, I'll tell you that."

Asked if such a statement wouldn't make him a target for every linebacker in the league, Bettis replied that he already was anyway.

Although some viewed his proclamation as a sign that his rookie season went to his head, Bettis was clearly trying to set high standards for a team sorely in need of leadership. "I feel I need to step up and say something," he explained. "I definitely can lead by example, too. I feel the situation has been put into my hands. I'll assume that responsibility."

There was little question that his stance produced immediate results for the team. By early October of '94, Bettis was working on a string of four 100-yard rushing games, and the Rams were showing signs of real life. Their 2-2 start included a 16-0 win over Joe Montana and the Kansas City Chiefs in which Bettis was a picture of ball-control precision.

But by the fifth game, a disappointing 8-5 loss to Atlanta, the Rams' passing game was in complete disarray and Bettis himself was taking a battering with a league-high 130 rushing attempts (26 carries per game).

"It's pretty tough right now because we haven't been very balanced on offense," he admitted at the time. "I'm happy to carry the load, but I'd be crazy to think I could go through another 11 games like this and still be able to play in this league for a number of years."

In retrospect, the downturn marked the end of the Rams' tenure in southern California. Bettis carried the ball 319 times that season under run-oriented coach Chuck Knox and racked up another 1,000-yard season. But the Rams were so deficient in so many areas. They finished the '94 campaign on a dismal note, fired Knox and moved their club to St. Louis, with the hope that coach Rich Brooks from the University of Oregon could turn their fortunes around.

Brooks favored a more wide-open attack, and Bettis promptly got on his bad side by holding out of training camp in 1995 in hopes of renegotiating his contract. What he got instead was a season of misery during which the Bus sat parked for long stretches. His number of carries plummeted to 183 that first year in St. Louis, and he finished with 637 yards rushing and only three touchdowns. Even worse, he came out of the season labelled as unhappy and a bit lazy, something Bettis would later blame on the organization.

Yet, as often is the case in pro sports, misery is the genesis of things good. The turnaround for Bettis came when the Rams dealt him to Pittsburgh before the '96 season for a pair of draft choices. Bettis considered the move something akin to drawing six perfect lotto numbers. First of all, he had gotten a taste of the Steelers' running schemes and fine offensive line play in the 1995 Pro Bowl. The experience left him wondering what he could do if he ever got to play in an offense like that. He soon found out.

His rushing attempts in 1996 rose to 320, and so did his yardage. He gained 1,431 yards and scored 11 TDs, which played a major factor in Pittsburgh claiming another AFC Central crown. Even better, the big showing prompted the Steelers to declare him their franchise building block and sign him to a four-year, $14.4 million contract extension. Yes, this was the same Pittsburgh organization that routinely let potential stars go to other teams rather than overspend on a contract. "When you look at the type of people we have around our locker room, he was a natural fit," Steelers coach Bill Cowher said of the Bus. "We approach a game with a no-nonsense attitude, and that's the way Jerome is. We have the type of people who recognize when it's time to work and when it's time to play."

Meanwhile, Brooks claimed that he made the trade because the Rams wanted more speed at running back. They drafted Lawrence Phillips from Nebraska but still could produce no better than a 6-10 finish that cost Brooks his job. Although paybacks weren't something Bettis was professing, he did have a point to prove when the two teams met in November of '96. He led the charge in a 42-6 rout with 129 yards rushing.

"Comments were made in St. Louis that I wasn't a game breaker, and the Rams wanted a game-breaking back," he told reporters afterward. "I wanted to show that I was more than just a bruiser, that I can also get the tough yards."

He emphasized that point in Pittsburgh's 42-14 defeat of the Indianapolis Colts in the first round of the playoffs. Bettis rushed for 102 yards, prompting Colts tackle Tony McCoy to observe, "He is going to pound and pound on you."

Unfortunately, Bettis carried a groin injury suffered against Indianapolis into the next playoff game against the New England Patriots, and the entire Steeler offense stalled in a 28-3 loss.

Regardless, the entire AFC had been put on notice that it was now on the Bus route.

"You better stop Bettis before he gets started," warned Ozzie Newsome, the Baltimore Ravens' player personnel vice president. "Once he gets through the line and squares up, he causes some problems for people. There aren't many people in the secondary who want to spend their Sunday afternoons tackling Jerome Bettis."

EARLY FIRE

As you might expect, Gladys Bettis isn't entirely pleased with her son's working environment. With eight brothers, she had to endure too much football growing up, from having the TV tied up by games on weekends to serving as an impromptu tackling dummy once too often. "I hated the sport," she said. "My brothers were extremely, extremely physical. I swore that I would not allow my children to play the game."

She did, however, love bowling. She and her husband made that sport a family activity that involved the children and kept them off the streets. Jerome, in fact, remains an avid bowler today (and even bowled a 300 game a couple of years ago), although he has trouble drumming up any interest among his NFL teammates.

As a youngster, though, his natural inclinations ran to the rough and tumble. He loved football. Bob Dozier, the longtime coach at Detroit's MacKenzie High, recalls looking up from his desk one day to see a "chiseled" 14-year-old, 190-pound Bettis asking to come out for the team.

As a sophomore, Bettis acquitted himself nicely as a noseguard and blocking back. He moved to runningback and linebacker his junior year. In one game, he nailed an opposing runningback so hard that the other team's coach told Dozier at halftime, "You better get that kid out of the game before he kills somebody."

But it was on offense that Bettis showed his real talent.

"He just loved to run over people," Dozier says. "Sometimes he'd have a guy beat but he'd slow down just so he could run him over. Defensive backs would look at him and think, 'This guy is slow,' until Jerome started pulling away from them. Those who caught him wished they hadn't because Jerome is just so physical."

If anything, the coaches had to encourage Bettis to juke and fake, to get away from defenders. He learned to do that well enough, and before long the Bettis running game had lifted long-struggling MacKenzie back to respect. The team advanced to the city championship game his senior year but lost when opposing Martin Luther King High spent the night keying on Bettis, a situation he sees as not unlike his frustrations in Los Angeles. "It was tough," he says, "because we didn't have enough quality players."

The loss, however, hardly dampened Bettis' intense competitive spirit. As the top-rated college prospect in Michigan, he made a big splash in both state and national all-star games that summer after his senior season. On two occasions, he found his all-star team behind at halftime. "He kicked the coaches out of the locker room and told his teammates he wasn't about to lose," Dozier recalls with a laugh. "He told them he didn't come there just to have fun and lose; he came to win."

"The guys weren't fighting," Bettis says. "I had to motivate 'em, get 'em rolling. I just didn't want them to give up. Something had to be said. In the heat of the battle, you just think of what needs to be done. Later you think, 'What made me do that?' "

Dozier obviously delights in the anecdote. "He's just so intense," the high school coach says. "Everything he does, he puts 100 percent into it. He has great leadership qualities. It gets everybody going because he's just so fiery. And there's nothing phony about it. You can see the fire in his eyes. Offensive linemen look at him and say, 'I gotta get the job done.'"

In fact, the offensive linemen blocking for him report that they feed off the intensity that builds in Bettis during a 100-yard rushing performance. "It's amazing how many defensive players get up slowly after Jerome hits them," former teammate Jackie Slater said. "He simply pounds and pounds on them. And you know what? He likes it."

"I get all fired up come game time," Bettis agrees. "I'm so pumped up I'm ready to burst. I just love playing this game. I love getting it going. I love running over people."

All of this, of course, stands in vast contrast to the image that Gladys Bettis holds of her sweet baby. But off the field he operates in a far kinder, gentler manner, evidenced by his frequent visits to his old high school.

By no means is MacKenzie located in Detroit's worst neighborhood. But there is gang and drug activity there. A few years ago, a track athlete from the school was killed in a drive-by shooting, Dozier reports, and another young football player—just about Bettis' size—was shot in the eye, and the bullet remains lodged there because doctors are fearful that removing it could cause more damage.

Because Bettis comes from a great family, because he was a talented athlete and a National Honor Society student, he could have used those advantages to go to one of Detroit's best high schools, Dozier says.

Instead, Bettis chose to remain in his neighborhood and become a shining example as a student athlete, whom MacKenzie principal Joseph Gilbert recalls was never late for class, was "always in the right place at the right time, always doing what he was supposed to be doing."

And now that he's a rising star in the NFL, he still returns frequently to MacKenzie, Dozier says. "Every time he's in town, he comes over here and spends a couple of hours. He talks to the students about leadership and grades. He always stresses academics first and takes great pride in having been an honor roll student. He's still the same down-to-earth Jerome that we knew."

"People who see me don't often associate me with books and academics," Bettis says. "I like to remind them that I care a lot about those things."

When he goes back to Detroit—where he spends the offseason in the new home he built for his family—Bettis says he seldom talks to the students at his old high school about the streets and drugs. Instead he turns to more positive things.

"I'm from where they're from," he says. "I don't try to tell them what to do. I try to help them out and give them a sense of direction in terms of decision making."

MacKenzie, however, remains a fresh reminder of the championship he didn't win, of what it feels like to be outmanned. It's a reminder he wants to carry with him in Pittsburgh because he believes he's now with a team that can finish off a season with a Super Bowl title.

Yes, it seems the sweet baby's fire is surely burning.

Which is bad news for all those defensive backs and linebackers out there. They know that they won't just feel his rumbling presence. They'll have to hear about it, too.

Chapter 9/Just Gimme The Damn Truth

Key let it be known that he wanted the damn ball.

et's get down to proper props from the gitgo on this one. Yessir, Keyshawn Johnson is da bomb. He may even be da shiznit someday, 'cause he's got the size (6-3, 215 pounds), the hands, the speed and a stone-cold killaz eye for the goal line. But writing about him ain't easy, uknowhatI'msayin'? It's not that he doesn't talk. He talks plenty. And he says plenty. But writing about Key is like writing about a young Charles Barkley, which is one reason I like Key, I really do. In fact, he and Charles are tight.

"That's my guy, that's my buddy," Keyshawn tells me, admitting to being a serious Barkley fan. It is mid-May, and we are talking in a bar in Myrtle Beach, South Carolina, of all places, where Keyshawn has come to "appear" for the celebrity golf tournament hosted by Oakland Raiders defensive lineman Chester McGlockton. I say "appear" because Key don't do golf, which is another reason I like him. I really do.

Big Chester is another of Key's buddies, which is a good idea. Because McGlockton is all square biz, a block of knock, with the skill to kill, uknowhatI'msayin'? No wide receiver in his right mind would turn down an invitation to be in McGlockton's golf tournament, even if it means traveling all the way across the country to South Carolina, where strangely enough, it's biker week at Myrtle Beach. The place is filled with thousands of bikers, profiling on their Harleys, sporting head rags and club colors and much black leather. They roll up and down the beach streets at all hours, the full-throated rumbling of their Harleys echoing off the

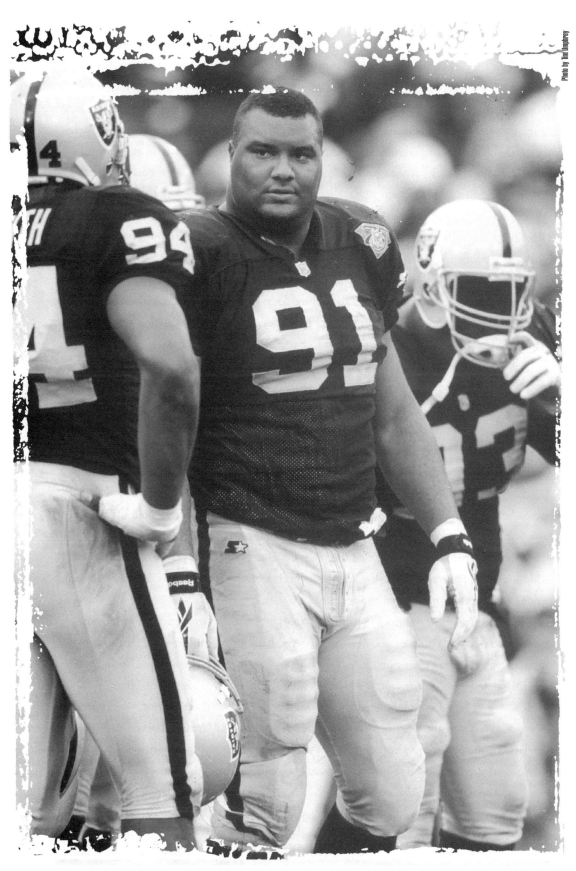

Photo by Tim Umphrey

When Chester McGlockton has a golf tournament, people attend.

high-rise walls. They sport Skulls 'n' Crossbones and Confederate flags and any other symbol of rebellion they can muster. An awful lot of 'em are yuppies — bankers and lawyers and real estate grifters — pretending to be bad on their weekends. The Hell's Angels are here, too, though. And the Pagans and the Outlaws as well as a number of truly dangerous people. Most of the meanest biker outlaws are either dead these days or in prison or both. However, there are enough bad asses still around to keep an edge to the gathering. Motels up and down the sprawling Myrtle Beach area are packed with bikers, which means the clerks and maids and maintenance men and managers all have nervous eyes.

Keyshawn, though, hardly feels ill at ease. He grew up on the streets of South Central L.A. and often made spare change working the crowds at L.A. Raider games. The tailgate parties around the Coliseum back then were packed with bikers and renegade types wearing head rags and black leather and menacing looks. Just the kind of people who might vote for Charles Barkley if he ever gets around to running for public office, as he sometimes threatens.

"He's one of my closer friends in terms of professional sports," Keyshawn says of Barkley. "I've been knowing Charles Barkley four or five years now."

"Has Charles told you the dangers of honesty?" I ask him.

Keyshawn gives me a look.

The reason I mention honesty is that Keyshawn has just gained much notoriety for his book, "Just Gimme The Damn Ball!" in which he fries the New York Jets organization and many of his coaches and teammates following the club's 1-15 finish in 1996. In the book, he pointed out some fairly obvious things, such as the dufus job Richie Kotite had done coaching the team. Johnson also suggested that offensive coordinator Ron Erhardt was somewhat imbecilic in his approach to guiding the unit; that high-priced quarterback Neil O'Donnell was "stiff" and had used injury as an excuse to miss some of the Jets' truly awful games. Johnson was particularly irritated that the offense focused on second-year receiver Wayne Chrebet. Johnson even implied that Chrebet, who is white, was the team's "mascot" who was featured in the offense for racial reasons.

The New York media and subsequently thousands of fans across the country were outraged by Keyshawn's commentary. "The title (of the book) itself indicates the receiver has a selfish streak and wasn't happy with his role as a pro," observed the Associated Press. Even Jets legend and broadcast analyst Joe Namath weighed in on the issue, telling reporters in New York that Johnson had violated an unwritten code by publicly criticizing a teammate. "Keyshawn has to realize it's not always his way," Namath said. "Until Keyshawn can accept the fact that he could be wrong or that he is wrong, he's going to have to struggle."

I find this widespread response to Johnson's book interesting. Many sportswriters today constantly complain that modern athletes have been coached so well in public relations that they never say what they really think, that they feed the media a constant diet of safe cliches. Here Johnson was, saying exactly what he thought, with no sugar-coating, and the media were enraged. Just like they used to get enraged when a young Charles Barkley would level a criticism at a nearby target.

I figured Charles might have warned Keyshawn about speaking out.

"Charles doesn't worry about it," Johnson tells me. "There's no danger in being honest. What danger is there in being honest?"

This last statement amazes me, because Keyshawn Johnson has grown up on the streets of South Central. He and his mother even lived out of a parked car for months at a time. "What danger is there in being honest?" he askes me.

"How can he be so naive? How can someone who grew up on the streets of South Central be so idealistic?" I ask myself. It doesn't quite make sense.

"Sometimes people can't handle your honesty, so they get mad at you," I tell him. "Sometimes honesty has a price."

"So what?" he asks, pointing out that he's tied tightly to the Jets contracturally. "My money's not guaranteed (most NFL contracts aren't). But I can't go anywhere. I got $7 million to sign (a cash bonus). That counts against the salary cap. I'm there at least until year five. That's pretty much guaranteed."

But, if the media write that you're a jerk, that makes the corporate people a little shy about using you as a product endorser. So being honest could cost you money, I tell him.

He points out that he was paid handsomely to speak his mind in his book. Which, of course, is true. Like Sir Charles and Dennis Rodman, Keyshawn has discovered that outrageousness can be profitable. "That's one deal," he says of the publishing contract. "I'm gonna move on and continue to do deals. That's just one deal. There's other deals to be done."

Yes, yes, other deals to be done. But honesty is a risky business. If they like your mouth, your style of outrageousness, you get to do much business. If they don't like it, well, ask Vernon "Mad Max" Maxwell how many endorsement deals he's inked recently.

On the other hand, Key doesn't act like somebody who decided to speak up just for the money. I remember watching Johnson on ESPN, being interviewed by Chris Meyer, who gave him the opportunity to take back some of the things said in his book. Keyshawn smiled politely and said, "Wait a minute, this is a free country, I'm entitled to my opinion." He coulda backed down, said the whole thing was a mistake, that he was misquoted. Charles, you may remember, tried that one, saying he was misquoted in his own book after it came out. Not a good thing to do. Key, though, didn't back down. No sell-out.

Whether he wants to admit it or not, being honest, doing things your way, comes with a price. I mention that people have dumped criticism on the Philadelphia 76ers' Allen Iverson, who like Keyshawn, was a top pick determined to do things his own way.

"Dumped on him for what?" Keyshawn says quickly. "Because he can score 40 points a game, and he can get a Reebok deal worth $5 million a year. And he can be the number one pick, and he can be himself and wear braids and shoot the ball and does not care what the older players are thinking because he's doing what he does best, and that's play basketball? Those older players didn't care about Allen Iverson when Allen Iverson was in jail (he was jailed for months for his part in a bowling alley brawl as a high schooler). The only person who gave a damn about him was (Georgetown) coach John Thompson and his family. The rest of them didn't care.

"Just like with me," he says. "Didn't nobody care about me when I slept in my car as a kid. They didn't reach out and grab me out of the seat and say, 'Well, come in my house where it's warm.' They didn't do that. So I don't give a damn about what they're saying now."

Speaking out also puts more pressure on him as a player, I tell him. It means he has to show up big time on the field.

"Keyshawn Johnson gotta perform no matter what," he says. "Gotta perform. 'Cause as far as everybody is concerned I didn't do anything last year, 'cause my team was 1-15. But I had 63 catches, 844 yards and eight touchdowns. For a rookie, if that ain't amazing, I don't know what is. Then what is? What other rookies do that? But that gets lost in 1-15."

I ask him if he has talked to other top draft picks about the pressures they face. "I haven't talked to them about it They know. They'll feel it. The heat. I got the pressure. When I was picked I was having the pressure to turn the Jets around. They put all of that on my shoulders. They put all of that on my shoulders and didn't let me turn 'em around.

"Isn't that crazy?" he asks me, looking for an answer.

And that, of course, is why Johnson criticized Wayne Chrebet. Because Johnson felt all the pressure as the number one pick in the draft, but he wasn't even the number one receiver on the worst team in the league. It was a major disrespect, one that wore on Johnson as the season dragged on and the situation got worse and worse.

I see top rookies get jerked around a lot in pro sports, I tell him.

"But why would you do that?" he asks me. "Why would you pick the number one, take the best player out of all of college football, and at the beginning of the season have him playing behind a guy who 29 other teams didn't even want at all, didn't even bring him in for a tryout."

Chrebet, of course, is primo proof that the NFL's equations don't always add up. He was an undrafted rookie free agent out of Hofstra (where the Jets hold their offseason camps). He was smallish and slow, yet he had this incredible knack for getting open and making the catch. In fact, Chrebet has caught 150 passes in his first two years in the league, more than any other receiver in the history of the game in his first two seasons.

One of Johnson's complaints is that, with his size and speed, Chrebet is not a "big-play" receiver, which is true. But then again, Chrebet led the league in 1997 in big plays, if you count third-down catches as big plays. He made 31 of 'em. *Sports Illustrated* quickly hammered these points in criticizing Keyshawn's book.

"I look at the *Sports Illustrated* article that came out, which was ridiculous," Johnson says.

"It was funny to me. Whatever. They go on to say that he outperformed me. That he had a better rookie season than I had. He played 16 games in a rookie season. I didn't."

He laughs, but it's a difficult laugh. Of all the points in his book, the ones about Chrebet draw the most heat. Most people would agree that his coaches obviously did a lousy job, that O'Donnell didn't have a great season. But Chrebet?

"Talking about how Chrebet couldn't play somewhere else, that's downright ignorant," Namath said flatly. "It would seem to me that Wayne is owed an apology and Keyshawn should be man enough to say, 'Hey, I made a mistake. This cat can play.'"

Former NFL great running back Eric Dickerson, also in town for McGlockton's tournament, has a different perspective: "Honesty is honesty," he tells me. "Some people don't like it. They can't accept. Some people are afraid to find out; other people are afraid to tell 'em."

Keyshawn isn't one of them, Dickerson says.

Chrebet and Johnson have adjacent lockers, and the former hasn't asked for an apology and the latter hasn't offered. In fact, they've hardly spoken.

O'Donnell, on the other hand, showed immediate anger when the book came out in the spring. The quarterback had come to the Jets as a multimillion dollar free agent from the Pittsburgh Steelers, but injuries meant that he appeared in only six games. Johnson insists there will be little long-term repercussions from his criticism.

Things, in fact, should be just fine, Johnson says, "once he learns the offense and he knows that I'm one of the players that he needs to get the ball to at all times to get this thing rolling in the right direction. I mean it's not a surprise that you got to get the ball in my hands. Stop acting surprised. Everybody's trying to act like it's a big surprise that I want the football. It's no surprise. You have to put the ball in my hands. If you don't put the ball in my hands, then we're gonna have some problems."

After saying that, Johnson confided that Raiders quarterback Jeff George, also something of an outspoken renegade, also here this weekend for McGlockton's golf outing, told him, "Keep saying what you're saying, because they need to get you the ball."

"I'm not backing down," Johnson says, his smile disappearing. "Neil O'Donnell has to come and throw me the ball; I have to catch it. I have to block for Wayne Chrebet; Chrebet has to block for me. Ron Erhardt has to help call the plays; I have to perform. The bottom line is, Keyshawn Johnson has to perform."

Even offseason conditioning workouts, where he had to share weight room time with the people he had just criticized, went quite well, he says. "We're lifting weights and stuff. It wasn't awkward at all. I didn't bat an eyelash. Didn't worry about it."

Finally he does admit, though, that people have a hard time with a rookie speaking out, that it goes against the grain of what athletes expect of younger teammates. But it's a shift that has come with Generation X, he says. "It's just a little bit different now. And, I think, as years go on people will get adapted to it. It's a new situation. I'm not the only rookie that speak out, and I'm not the only rookie that people consider a radical, or whatever the case is. I don't think I'm radical. I think I tell it like it is, and there's no sugar-coating. Just plain and simple, everybody across the board know, who the top two receivers on the team should be. Me and Jeff Graham. There's no question about it."

If nothing else, I tell Keyshawn, weathering this criticism will make you stronger.

"Very strong," he says. "That's why I don't pay attention to the New York media. I basically let them do their job, and I smile after they do their job. They will break certain athletes. Me, they don't break. I smile at 'em everyday. Get in my truck and go home.

"It doesn't bother me," he tells me. "Everything I said in my book, it's there. It's there. That's what it was. That's the way it was for me as a rookie, and that's the way it was for me growing up. So you move forward from there. We're trying to get going in the football season of '97. That stuff's in '96. ... It's time to move on now."

The one person he does have to pay attention to is new Jets coach Bill Parcells, the stern taskmaster who drove players in New England to distraction while driving them to the Super Bowl. The tough talk, though, is just fine with Keyshawn. In a few days, he'll arrive at the team's first minicamp only to have Parcells complain that he is overweight. Instead of complaining, Johnson will quietly lose the weight and get ready to play. It's obvious that Parcells has his immediate respect, because the coach's presence means an end to the dismal losing.

"Parcells runs this ship," he tells me. "Thumbs up. We moving all the way together, me 'n him. As he goes down, I go down. As I rise, he rises."

But Parcells is defensive-oriented guy, I point out.

"Doesn't matter," he says. "I'm a player. He can be defensive-minded all he wants to be. He knows that I'm a player, and I know that he's a coach. I know he's a good coach, and he knows I'm a damn good player. So it doesn't matter. I could be a kicker. It doesn't matter, I'm a player. If I was a hell of a kicker and made 15 in a row, you don't think he wouldn't like for me to kick for him?

"I think Coach Parcells and his staff know who the players are who can help this team win. Rather than sitting around in a pattern of way, showing sympathy to somebody for something other than football."

I wince. There he goes again, referring to Chrebet. On the other hand, it takes a lot of honesty to turn a 1-15 team around. People have to say what they think. More than that, they have to do something about it. I mention a core of leadership is needed to build a team.

"If I'm not a leader, then I don't know who is," Keyshawn says emphatically. "I'm really excited going into the season. I'm so excited it's unbelievable. I don't even care about 1-15. That's last year. That don't mean anything to me. I'll never be 1-15 again on any other team I play on in my career. And that's kind of a guarantee."

Kind of a guarantee? That must be more of the Barkley in him. As we talk, the Houston Rockets are preparing to do battle on the tube. If the Rockets keep winning in the NBA playoffs, then Keyshawn plans to head to Houston to watch his friend/mentor courtside.

"Charles has promised they'll win," Key tells me, sounding a little doubtful. "But you don't take that as a reporter and go with it. You know how that goes."

Yes, I know how that goes. Start promising wins and wind up losing. But I also know Charles. He'll do anything to try and fire his team up.

"Charles Barkley don't care," Key tells me proudly, smiling his 25-year-old smile. "He's gonna say, gonna do what he has to do."

Part III The Team Thang

Lombardi, the ultimate dynasty man.

hina's great succession of dynasties lasted roughly 4,000 years. The Han, for example, ruled for about a millenium, while the Sung, the Ming and Ch'ing each chugged along for three centuries, give or take a decade or two. Obviously, when we talk about "dynasties" in American professional sports, we're engaging in more than a bit of hyperbole. But, heck, what good are games if you can't talk 'em up?

Within the 77-year history of the National Football League there are a select few teams that have been so good and won so many championships that we've been moved to declare them dynastic. Immediately, the Cleveland Browns of the 1940s and '50s come to mind, as do the Green Bay Packers of the '60s, the Pittsburgh Steelers of the '70s, and the San Francisco 49ers of the '80s and '90s.

It's too bad Dallas Cowboys owner Jerry Jones didn't take the time to look closely at these great teams of the past. If he had, maybe he wouldn't have been so hasty about chasing off coach Jimmy Johnson a few seasons back. A review of the NFL's most dominant teams over the years reveals they've all been commanded by a brilliant, hard-driving coach, the kind who casts his team in the mold of his own fierce personality. Because he's so intense, the dynastic coach is usually feared and hated and loved.

Sometimes the coach of a dynasty depends heavily on star players, but more often than not he prefers to settle for smart, talented men who can execute his system. Take, for instance, Paul Brown of the great Cleveland Browns. His personality was so strong, the owners even named the team after him! Obviously, it takes more than coaching to build a dynasty. One thing that made Paul Brown such a great coach was his eye for talent.

Today, the challenge is even greater. Not only do you have to find the talent, you have to keep it. And free agency makes that very problematic. If you don't believe that, look how quickly the Cowboys, the supposed rulers of the '90s, have lost key players to other teams offering better deals. The circumstances are so dire that some observers say that modern sports dynasties are a thing of the past. Who knows for sure? If they are, that's all the more reason to take a little stroll down the NFL's memory lane to look at a few of those great teams. Are you paying attention, Jerry?

THE BROWNS

The Browns are the quintessential dynasty. They began life in 1946 in the upstart All-America Football Conference, which was set up to rival the NFL. Four years later, three teams from the AAFC—the Browns, the 49ers and the Baltimore Colts—would merge with the NFL. But from 1946 to '49 the two leagues ran a hot competition for players and fans. Actually the financial competition between the leagues was a lot better than that in the new league. The Browns easily ruled it, winning all four AAFC league titles.

The NFL's bosses scoffed and told reporters that the AAFC was simply an inferior league. But when the leagues merged in 1950, the Browns promptly claimed the NFL title, too. In fact, in their first six years in the NFL, the Browns played their way into the league championship game six times and won three titles, making for seven league titles in 10 seasons and a second-place finish the other three times. Their regular season record from 1946 to 1955 was 105-17-4. Not bad for the first decade of operation of an "expansion" team and a coach who had never worked in pro football.

"Paul was ahead of his time in terms of teaching and organization," said Ara Parseghian, the great Notre Dame coach who played for Brown. "But the singleness of purpose is what Paul brought to coaching—that football wasn't just a job but something you gave your life to."

Brown came from the cradle of the game, Massillon (Ohio) High School, where he played and later coached the team to an 80-8-2 record. From there he went to Ohio State and won a national championship in 1942. When World War II broke out, he coached football at the U.S. Naval Training Station in Great Lakes, Illinois, where he spent two years experimenting with different football philosophies.

When the Browns hired him after the war, he knew exactly what he wanted, and much of that included a list of players he had either coached or coached against over the years. First on the list was Otto Graham, who had played tailback at Northwestern. Brown knew he would make a great quarterback, able to throw on the run going to his right or left, able to make those perfect touch passes or push the ball long, whatever the offense needed. To go with him, Brown added great receivers Mac Speedie and Dante Lavelli, who were able to burn through their patterns with great precision.

For power out of the backfield, Brown turned to 6-1, 240-pound Marion Motley, a cunning bruiser. Tackle Lou Groza and linebacker Bill Willis drove the defense, while center Grank Gatski was the force on the offensive line. All of them were Hall of Fame performers.

Brown's intense approach meant that the club's greatness grew far beyond game performances. "Eleven of the first 23 Super Bowls were won by guys who played for Paul or who coached under him," Dante Lavelli once noted. "Chuck Noll has won four, Bill Walsh three, Don Shula two, Weeb Ewbank one, Don McCafferty one." Two of those coaches—Noll and Walsh—created dynasties of their own, a testimony to the fact that Brown's methods weren't just ahead of their time: They were for the ages.

GREEN BAY PACKERS

Where Paul Brown molded an expansion team into a power, Vince Lombardi scooped up the dregs of the league to fashion his model of gridiron excellence. Once upon a time the Green Bay Packers had been great, but they finished 1-10-1 in 1958 and seemed doomed to small-market failure. Then Lombardi arrived on the scene with his fundamental credo: "Winning isn't everything. It's the only thing."

In reality, his world was a little broader than that, but not much. He told associates he placed God and family before football. A devout Catholic, he took communion each day. "If you ever heard him talk, you knew why he had to go to church every day," Packers quarterback Bart Starr once quipped about Lombardi's legendary profanity. The coach would use his acid speech to scald the hide off any player who didn't die Packer green and gold every minute of every game and every practice.

This approach produced astonishing results. For 1959, Lombardi turned the hapless Packers into a 7-5 team. The next season, they played for and narrowly lost the league championship to the Philadelphia Eagles. It would be Lombardi's last loss in a championship game.

Between 1961 and 1967, he won five NFL titles and two Super Bowls, with his teams compiling a regular-season record of 74-20-4. Bringing a religious-like fervor to his job, Lombardi preached excellence, toughness and winning, and never failed to turn his explosive temper on any player who failed to pay the physical price. "He sold it," Starr once said of Lombardi's philosophy. "Everybody bought it."

From Starr, the 17th-round draft pick who fashioned himself into a leader, to defensive anchor Willie Davis, they all came away believing in Lombardi's approach. When Starr passed, he had receivers Carroll Dale, Max McGee, Marv Fleming and Boyd Dowler waiting to make big plays. But most of the time the Packers relied on a no-frills ground game. With Jim Taylor and Paul Hornung as running backs, and Jerry Kramer, Forrest Gregg, Jim Ringo and Fuzzy Thurston doing the blocking, the Packers took opponents wide with powerful sweeps, then hammered down the middle. "Run to daylight" was Lombardi's creed, and the offense created plenty of that.

The defense, meanwhile, dealt out nothing but darkness, with Davis at end, crazy men Ray Nitschke, Lee Roy Caffey and Bill Forester at linebacker, Henry Jordan at tackle and Herb Adderley and Willie Wood in the secondary. The coach made sure they all performed at their peak.

"Lombardi never let up, man," said Hall of Famer Nitschke, often the target of the coach's furious temper. "He never let up."

PITTSBURGH

Chuck Noll spent his playing days running plays in and out as a guard in Paul Brown's Cleveland offense. In 1969, at age 37, he was named head coach of the Pittsburgh Steelers, a team that had enjoyed just eight winning seasons in its previous 36 years of operation. "We will change history," Noll promised his first day on the job.

He never quite accomplished that, of course, but he did amazing things with the team's present and future, beginning with his very first draft selection, defensive tackle Mean Joe Greene out of North Texas State. Also in that '69 draft was defensive end L.C. Greenwood.

A year later came quarterback Terry Bradshaw and cornerback deluxe Mel Blount. Linebacker Jack Ham was the prize of the '71 draft, along with safety Mike Wagner and defensive linemen Ernie Holmes and Dwight White. From 1972, the Steelers harvested running back Franco Harris. But 1974 was the best of all, bringing receivers Lynn Swann and John Stallworth, linebacker Jack Lambert and center Mike Webster.

"Weapons," was how the young coach described his draft picks. Did we mention that they were loaded?

The first sign of this actually came in December 1972 when Harris made "The Immaculate Reception" that defeated the Oakland Raiders and gave the Steelers the first playoff win in their long, miserable history. It was obvious the team's fortunes had changed. The major key was the "Steel Curtain" defense, led by Greene and his cohorts on the line.

By January 1975, Noll and his Steelers claimed their first Super Bowl, a 16-6 thumping of the Minnesota Vikings. Over the next five seasons, they would add three more Super Bowl titles, including two victories over the Dallas Cowboys. The Steelers' fourth title came in 1979, over the Los Angeles Rams. Through it all, Noll maintained a low-key, intense approach. "Winning a fourth Super Bowl should put us in a special category," Blount said in '79. "I think this is the best team ever assembled. They talk about Vince Lombardi, but I think the Chuck Noll era is even greater."

49ERS

The San Francisco 49ers' run of championships, a total of five stretching between 1981 and 1995, makes for what some consider the most impressive dynasty, because the faces keep changing but the wins just keep coming. First there was Bill Walsh with Joe Montana calling the signals, throwing to receivers Freddie Solomon and Dwight Clark. They won Super Bowl XVI over Cincinnati in 1981, with rookies Ronnie Lott, Eric Wright and Carlton Williamson working the secondary and veteran Fred Dean revving up the pass rush.

Three seasons later, in 1984, they won it again, after adding running back Roger Craig and linebacker Keena Turner from the draft. From the 1985 draft came plum receiver Jerry Rice, and 1986 brought fullback Tom Rathman, receiver John Taylor and defensive lineman Charles Haley.

Sufficiently recharged, the 'Niners claimed two more Super Bowl championships in '88 and '89, only Walsh wasn't there to enjoy the fourth title, having relinquished his head coaching duties to George Seifert, his top assistant. The system stayed the same, only the names and numbers changed. Even backup quarterback Steve Young made key appearances in the drive to Super Bowl XXIV.

The 1990 season brought a narrow miss at a three-peat. San Francisco finished the season with a league-best 14-2 mark but lost 15-13 to the New York Giants in the NFC championship game. When age and injury began to slow Joe Montana, Young moved in to claim three straight league passing titles.

Heading into the 1994 campaign, they showed the pedigree of a legitimate dynasty. Over the course of Walsh's and Seifert's tenure they had stacked up a 170-84-1 record. But Young still hadn't quarterbacked a Super Bowl championship team. That, of course, changed in January 1994. San Francisco defeated the San Diego Chargers to take that fifth Super Bowl title, moving them a notch ahead of Pittsburgh among the "modern" teams. But their record still doesn't approach the Browns' touchstone of seven championships in 10 seasons. Some fans might argue that those old Cleveland records don't count, because they didn't play "modern" football. But that's why we call them dynasties, isn't it?

Because they go back a long, long time.

With that in mind, we'll spend the last part of this book looking at four different NFL teams — the Green Bay Packers, who have just collected one more Super Bowl title and are trying to follow it up with another; the Dallas Cowboys, who are struggling to regain their Super Bowl form; and the expansion franchises of the Jacksonville Jaguars and Carolina Panthers, new teams that are proving they don't want to wait around to compete.

Chapter 10/Cat Fight!
The Jaguars And Panthers Have Clawed Their Way To The Top In A Hurry

Photo by Scott Cunningham

The NFL's young black catz are ready to growl.

As shiny new football teams in the salty old National Football League, theirs is a natural rivalry. At the starting gate two seasons ago, they sneered at each other and declared they were headed in different directions.

The Carolina Panthers were determined to live for the moment, to cash in draft picks for seasoned veterans, to compete now and worry about everything else later.

The Jacksonville Jaguars, the other franchise, said that they were going for youth and building a big tomorrow through the draft.

Funny, here they both sit two seasons later having arrived at the same destination, and both of their tomorrows look awfully rosy. For that matter, the present ain't bad either.

The Panthers enter the fall as the reigning NFC West Division champions, having dispensed with the storied San Francisco 49ers and Dallas Cowboys in a late-season run last year that carried them almost over the rainbow, just one win shy of a trip to the Super Bowl.

The Jags took an almost identically exhilirating ride, pulling their season from the ashes of a dismal 4-7 start, to steam along through seven straight wins, dumping Denver and Buffalo in playoff road games before seeing their dream dissipate in the AFC championship game against New England. They, too, could see the klieg lights of the Super Bowl glittering on the horizon. Close enough, you might say, to hear the bands playing.

The stunning performance of both teams has sent shock waves through the NFL. Already the older franchises are complaining that the league allowed these '90s expansion teams huge helpings of draft picks and free agents to make them immediately competitive. For many pro sports power brokers, it was embarrassing to see the NFL's proudest teams upstaged by upstarts. And it wasn't just pride that got hurt. When coach Dom Capers Panthers won the NFC West with a 7-1 divisional record, the other four coaches in the division lost their jobs.

FLUKE?

Was their success a freak occurrence? That question will beg an answer when both teams resume competition this fall.

The thought of that has at least crossed the mind of Carolina quarterback Kerry Collins.

"I think we're gonna go back every year," Collins said of his team's trip to the top, "because I made it my second year. But of course it's not that way."

He knows that in the wake of the big season, expectations will be gigantic, Collins said. "But I think it's a little bit unrealistic of our fans. I don't want to say they're spoiled. I speak for myself, too. I don't think I realize just how special it was that we did make it that far."

When he does stop to ponder it, Collins thinks of Dan Marino, who got to the Super Bowl as a young quarterback and never made it back.

Yet there's no question that both of these clubs have the talent level to be good for a very long time, if they can hold onto their chemistry in the age of free agency. In that regard, Carolina may actually have an edge, although both teams have made excellent personnel decisions.

What hurts the Jaguars is coach Tom Coughlin's image as a strict disciplinarian, which has some observers predicting that Jacksonville will have trouble attracting the best free agents year after year. Coughlin disputes that as just so much poppycock, although there's no question that he began to lighten up on his myriad of team rules his second season.

Such speculation, of course, only fuels the intense competition between the two clubs. It galls the Jags to no end that they won four games in the first season of existence, more than any other expansion team in NFL history, and nobody noticed.

The reason for that obviously is because the Panthers won seven games that same first season, thus putting the Jaguars in the back seat from the start. It was then that Jags management began suggesting that the competition between the two expansion teams was a tortoise and hare race, which they, the Jags, would eventually win with patience.

Kerry Collins is always ready to go up top.

"We obviously spent the year in the development of the young players, whether it be rookies or first-year players," Coughlin said smugly at the time. "That's how we chose to develop our football team. Not that youth is the absolute answer. But outstanding ability, combined with youth and good experience, are a good combination."

Certainly the Panthers' blitzing defense was a big reason for their success last year, yet the age of their linebacking corps, led by Sam Mills and Kevin Greene, was also cited as one of their weaknesses.

Yet no sooner had observers begun playing the age question with Carolina then General Manager Bill Polian answered with the signing of highly regarded free agent linebacker Micheal Barrow and defensive end Ray Seals (although they later lost Greene in a contract dispute).

"The Panthers are going to be Super Bowl contenders not only this year," trumpeted *Football News*, "but for the next five or 10 years."

HIGH PROFILE

While both teams have based much of their progress on building excellent defensive units, it is their young quarterbacks who have stepped into the public eye as high-profile leaders.

For Jacksonville, that would be Mark Brunell, a stocky six-foot lefthander with a scrambling style and understated religious conviction that brings to mind San Francisco's Steve Young.

He came to the Jaguars just hours before the 1995 draft having played in just two NFL games and thrown 27 passes as a backup for the Green Bay Packers. Jacksonville coach and GM Tom Coughlin had spent months looking for the QB with the arm, toughness and smarts to run his club.

At first, Brunell had a mighty tough time learning to stand in the pocket and pass. As Brunell got better, the Jags got better, leading to their dramatic improvement down the stretch in 1996. Now, the Jaguars have to pinch themselves because they gave up only a third- and fifth-round pick for the star in the making.

"Mark Brunell is going to be the best quarterback in the league," former teammate Andre Rison predicted. "Mark is going to be the man."

That dream, it seems, has come true sooner than later.

When last season was over, Brunell stood atop the league in passing yards, having rung up 4,367. He also led the NFL's quarterbacks in rushing, having picked up 396 yards on 80 carries. To top it off, he added Pro Bowl MVP honors last year.

Across the league, the reviews were rave. "We've never faced a quarterback like that before," Denver's Alfred Williams said after Brunell led the upset of the Broncos.

That's quite an accomplishment for a guy who wasn't even the top quarterback from his school taken in the draft (Billy Joe Hobert was taken ahead of him). But that didn't matter.

Getting drafted late meant that Brunell got to spend two seasons in Green Bay where he was able to observe the thriving spirituality of defensive end Reggie White. "He's a great man," Brunell says.

In Jacksonville, Brunell worked diligently with offensive coordinator Kevin Gilbride (who has since moved on as the head coach of the San Diego Chargers). "His growth is as profound as anybody's I've been around," Gilbride said of Brunell. "He's trying to make a much more difficult development now, to be the kind of precise, mistake-free quarerback the greats are."

In 1996, he threw 20 interceptions and 19 touchdowns, but the mistakes all but disappeared as Brunell guided the Jags on their winning streak at the end of the schedule.

Even so, the Jags' playoff opportunity came down to a piece of luck, when Morten Anderson, Atlanta's veteran placekicker, missed a 30-yard chip shot at the end of the last regular-season game that enabled Jacksonville to get into the playoffs.

Feeling a little goofy, the Jags decided to invite Anderson to present Brunell with his team MVP award at an offseason banquet. Another kicker might have taken the invitation as a dig, but Anderson surprisingly accepted, saying, "Hey, I'm over it, so why not? I think it'll be fun."

Brunell's Carolina counterpart is Collins, who was thrown into a starting role shortly after joining the club as a rookie in 1995. His first campaign was understandably marked by ups and downs, but one thing emerged: Collins' size and strength (he's 6-5, 240) began to create problems for other teams. Whereas in the past, pro scouts had considered too much size a liability for a QB prospect, they began to revise their thinking.

"Probably my strength is that I stand strong in the pocket," Collins admitted in an interview over the summer. "I like to think that I can make most of the throws. Really, I think leadership is a big part of it, and I think I have that quality."

He says he's proud that his performance has scouts re-evaluating bigger quarterbacks. "I always wanna make sure that I don't get too big...," he jokes, adding that if he did he could wind up playing guard.

"I think it helps," he said of the size. "The guys across the ball are getting bigger and stronger and faster. You gotta be able to absorb the hits. I like to think that because I'm bigger, I have a little easier time doing that."

Although he missed four games in 1996 with injuries, his record as a starter for the season was 9-3. In one stretch of 26 quarters, he threw just two interceptions.

Nearing his 24th birthday, Collins came up with his biggest game in a key road win at San Francisco, throwing for 327 yards and three touchdowns on 22-of-37 passing in a 30-24 victory that propelled Carolina into the divisional lead.

It also earned him honors as the NFC offensive player of the week.

"It just so happened that it was a big game," he says now, "and we threw the ball quite a

Brunell zipped for better than 4,000 yards in '96.

bit. I was able to do some good things. It was a fun game."

A fun game?

The 49ers didn't think so. They were stompin' around, spittin' and swearin' and disrespectin' the Panthers. Collins, though, just stood in there and refused to back down.

Having come through so much last year, he was despondent after the Panthers' season came to an end against Green Bay in the NFC title game.

"It was pretty painful," he said. "I mean, you play the whole year, and it's such a long season. And you're right there. You can see the Super Bowl in your grasp.

"I've gotten over it, I guess. I don't know if you ever really get over it. It's always in the back of your mind. What could have been, that sort of thing. But this year's another year. It doesn't matter what you did last year. It's a whole new season."

Asked what he learned from the process, Collins answered quickly. "Home field definitely helps. That's one thing I learned last year. Home field is key. Hopefully, we'll get it this year."

There, in that one sentence, you have the essence of what has the rest of the NFL fussing about these expansion teams. They're not just glad to have made a trip to the conference championship game. Now they're talking about home field advantage!

Like it or not, the league's older teams better get used to it. These upstart cats have snuggled in at the top. They like it. And they're here to stay.

Dom Capers runs the show in Carolina.

Chapter 11/God Bless Texas

Photo by Tim Umphrey

remember dropping in on the Dallas Cowboys a few years back, at the height of their heyday, before their silver stars got tarnished, before the weirdness settled on this team like the scent of a dead skunk hanging over a hot August day.

It was a Monday afternoon in their locker room at Valley Ranch, the aftermath of yet another victory. Once again the forces of evil had been turned back, and the Cowboys had survived. For a few hours, the Buddy "Blowhard" Ryans of the world, the perpetrators of head-bashing, career-ending blitzes, had been minimized.

The day before, it had been the defensive rush that made the Cowboys wary. But on that Monday, it was the media crush that they had to face. Another week, another big game lay ahead, and there were questions to be answered. About two dozen reporters, armed with cameras, microphones and notebooks, were waiting to catch the stars before a 2 p.m. team meeting.

Quarterback Troy Aikman suddenly appeared, eyed the gathering with his usual contempt, and in a swift move ducked the rush and slipped out of the room. Running back Emmitt Smith took a different strategy—he waited until just four minutes before the meeting to make his appearance, leaving the media a little frantic. They hustled to encircle Smith for questions about his nagging hamstring injury. The scramble prompted offensive tackle Nate Newton to jump on the locker room P.A. system and announce that Smith should wear a condom while conducting interviews.

The adulation for the Cowboys has always been a bit cloying. But the questions were much easier to answer in those good old days, before Michael Irvin fell from grace and the organization stumbled under the weight of one public relations disaster after another.

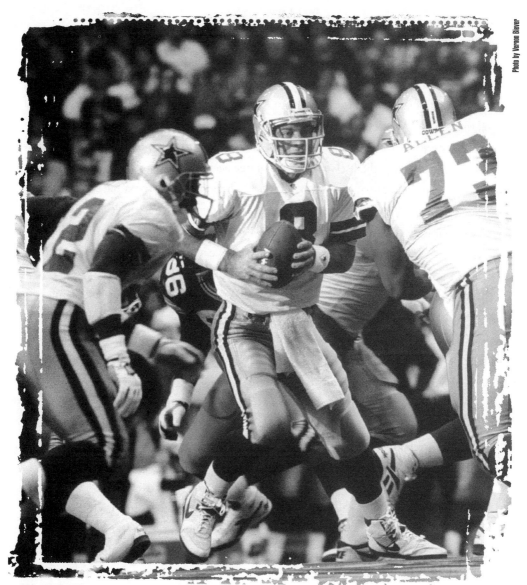

Photo by Vernon Biever

Aikman to Emmitt.

I remember Emmitt Smith that afternoon, grinning broadly, the diamond stud in his ear glistening in the TV lights. He offered up reassurances that his hamstring was okay, which was very, very big news in Dallas at the time, bigger, say, than funding for supercollider projects or the latest polls from the governor's race.

This, after all, was football-crazy Texas in its greatest hour of gridiron glory. The Cowpokes had just won two consecutive Super Bowls, and the only thing seemingly standing between them and a run of three or four of the suckers was good health. At the time, it all seemed to hinge on a hamstring, yet, in retrospect, it seems clear now that it was far more fragile than that.

At the time, the team was driven by its trinity of offensive superstars—Smith, Aikman and Irvin—who gave them a legitimate shot at becoming the first National Football League team to win three straight Super Bowls.

The thought of this three-peat had fans in every corner of Cowboyland, which reaches far beyond the boundries of the Lone Star state, twisting their intensity up another notch.

Yet, as crazy as their fans were, no one wanted this third title—no one sensed the urgency more—than the Cowboys themselves. The age of free agency had just dawned, meaning that players would come and players would go, all to the wherefores of the next big contract, surely threatening the Cowboys' opportunity to sustain a dynasty. "Since we're all together and this may be our last time, hell, let's make this the best run we've ever had," Smith said that day. "Let's do it the way it's supposed to be done. We have an opportunity for three Super Bowls, and I want to think this was the best team ever."

Clouding the picture back then was a controversial coaching change that had many observers thinking the Cowboys' glory train had been derailed. In a fit of bar room anger, owner Jerry Jones had fired immensely successful coach Jimmy Johnson, despite the fact that they were old friends and teammates from the University of Arkansas, despite the fact that Johnson had just coached Dallas to two big trophies.

Stepping into the wake of this calamity were new head coach Barry Switzer and new offensive coordinator Ernie Zampese, both of whom grinned and guffawed at the pressure. Could the newly rebuilt defense stand up to the challenges week after week? Could the offense stay healthy? Could Switzer provide the discipline that a team soaked in adulation would need?

The circumstances themselves were enough to drive a wedge between the churlish Aikman and his back-slapping new head coach, whose last coaching experience had been watching the disintegration of the University of Oklahoma program that he had guided to national prominence. If Switzer seemed a little confused at early key moments on the Cowboys sideline, Aikman had been there before, so rather than waiting for a coaching decision, he simply took charge. If Switzer chaffed at these or other small indignities wrought by doing the bidding of Jones, the coach was a master at not showing it. Amazingly, he seemed unconcerned that he would surely be the fall guy if the team chemistry fell apart.

Fortuitously, Aikman predicted, "There will come a time when Barry will have to take a stand."

Yes, the quarterback was, for the record, setting the responsibility squarely on the coach's shoulders. Not that Aikman didn't do everything possible, including playing through a series of career-threatening head injuries that would leave him struggling with bouts of memory lapse for seasons to come.

Free agency had brought the loss of John Gesek and Kevin Gogan from the offensive line

Switzer can sit on the hot seat and still grin.

and coordinator Norv Turner to a head coaching job in Washington and tackle Erik Williams to auto accident injuries. As a result, Aikman found himself that season yelling at a rookie lineman here or there for missed assignments that resulted in the quarterback getting levelled by the pass rush.

For the immensely popular Irvin, the main adversity wasn't injury or even the zone and double-coverage defenses that were determined to take away the Cowboys' long-ball threat. Mainly, his struggle each evening came down to which delicious elements of the Dallas night life he wanted to sample. The choices were bodacious.

Neon means coverage with style.

That didn't mean that Irvin didn't have his on-field problems in those days. The 1994 season was a month-old before the big-playing, big-talking receiver had caught his first touchdown pass, mainly because of the defenses gearing their efforts to shutting him down. The circumstances had tested the 6-2, 208-pound Irvin, who in college nicknamed himself "Playmaker." There were early season scenes from the Dallas sideline with him storming about and swearing that he was being overlooked in the offense.

"I don't tolerate that," Aikman reacted angrily. "Mike should be wise enough to know we'll get him the ball."

Outside of that, the Cowboys seemed their smiling, assured selves that Monday in 1994, the darlings of Dallas. Behind the scenes the forces that would take them down gathered momentum. On the surface, only one question seemed to matter: Could the team's offensive superstars withstand the battering that opposing defenses subjected them to week after week?

"That's something I can't worry about," Smith said, "because if I do, I end up shortchanging myself."

For Aikman, the issue centered on a series of six concussions dating back through several seasons and their long-term effects. Get enough concussions and risk permanent brain damage, doctors had repeatedly warned pro football players. That fall Cardinals' linebacker Wilber Marshall sent Aikman to the sideline with a hammering blow to the chin that caused yet another concussion.

"I find myself forgetting things," he would later reveal. "I don't know if it's like anyone else forgetting things, or if it's the result of being hit in the head too much. I forget having entire conversations with people."

Despite the risks, Aikman had missed one game, then rushed back to his starting role the next week, much as Smith had made a point of battering through a playoff win the previous December against the Giants, despite a separated shoulder that would require offseason surgery.

That, as much as anything, separated the Cowboys from the competition. In addition to their bountiful talent and competitiveness, the Dallas offensive stars have shown a ready willingness to risk their long-term health to keep winning.

The immense risks seemed to steep Aikman's resentment of the underprepared Switzer. The situation intensified with their failure to win that third consecutive championship that winter of 1995, their hopes of a dynasty derailed by injuries and a lack of depth. They simply arrived at the playoffs too beat up to outlast the competition.

In the wake of that disappointment, Jones turned to the courting of San Francisco defensive back "Neon" Deion Sanders, the ostentatious "Prime Time," a fitting nickname in that he was the league's most intimidating coverage/return man. His presence solidified the Dallas defense and allowed the Cowboys to wrest the Super Bowl title back from the 49ers in February 1996. For that brief instant, Jones and Switzer were vindicated. God had blessed

Aikman, Smith, Irvin & Associates with three titles in four seasons, and the future seemed Texas-sized and packed with limousines, longnecks and gorgeous blondes.

But it all disintegrated just a few weeks later when Dallas police busted into a Marriott Residence Inn room and caught Irvin in a drugs and sex scandal that would blast the good times away like a twister rolling in off the nearby plain.

Eventually, the whole thing would be laid at Switzer's feet, driven by Aikman's haunting prediction that, someday, the coach would indeed have to take a stand. Switzer would have gladly done so, if he had only known which one to take.

The pressure built as the team's prospects disintegrated over the 1996 season, with Irvin suspended for the first five games. They still managed to finish the year at 10-6 and make the playoffs. But the image of the Cowpokes in their final hours of the 1996 season wasn't pretty. Contained by the Carolina Panthers' intimidating defense in the NFC semifinals, the Dallas offense was short on receivers and answers. Some would say that was to be expected considering that this team spent the year embroiled in one drug-related controversy after another.

"We lost Michael Irvin for five games, Kelvin Martin and Kevin Williams were hobbled by injuries, Jay Novacek was gone, Eric Bjornson was limping on two sprained ankles, and Deion (Sanders) never got into the flow," Aikman said. "Our offense was an embarrassment and I was horrible."

Aikman pointed out that a dozen other NFL teams would kill for a 10-6 finish. In Dallas, though, the expectations are dramatically steeper than that.

No one has come to understand that better than Switzer. No sooner had the Cowboys issued new vows to clean up their act for 1997 and hired former great Calvin Hill (father of the NBA's Grant Hill) as a consultant to help them do it than Switzer was caught toting an unlicensed gun into an airport. Considering the team's public relations nightmares, Jones was tempted to fire him but settled instead for a league-record $75,000 fine.

That was followed by a charge by Nate Newton's former girlfriend that he had sexually assaulted her (a grand jury later declined to indict him on the charge).

If nothing else, the incidents emphasized to Jones and his minions that they must find a way to scrub the tarnish off the team's silver stars. The fastest way to accomplish that would be a return to championship contention in 1997. Anything less meant that the proceedings would play out in the Texas media like a smarmy B-grade Western. Heaven knows the city had seen enough of prime time soap operas.

One of the keys to turning the thing around included finding some way around the team's severe decline in manpower. Since the end of the 1996 campaign, the Cowboys had seen seven unrestricted free agents leave for other teams. In addition, back injuries caused tight end Jay Novacek and defensive end Charles Haley, both former Pro Bowlers, to retire. The free agent losses included both kickers (punter John Jett to Detroit and placekicker Chris Boniol to Philadelphia). Even worse, Darrin Smith, the team's most effective linebacker,

Photo by Vernon Biever

Playmaker got game.

headed to Philadelphia, and two other starters, wide receiver Kevin Williams and safety George Teague, also went to other teams.

In the five years since the NFL had been forced to allow free agency, the Cowboys had lost 33 players, including 14 starters and three Pro Bowlers. The team had managed to prosper despite those losses largely because of the performances of its big stars. For it to right itself again, Jones' club would need big seasons from all of them, especially Irvin.

PLAYMAKER

"Can I tell you who I am?" Irvin supposedly asked the cops as they were about to arrest him on cocaine and pot charges in March 1996, just days before his 30th birthday.

Little need for that.

All of Texas knows him as the Playmaker, the name he gave himself as a gold-chain wearing, trash-talking star for Jimmy Johnson at the University of Miami back in 1987. He is one of the grandaddies of attitude, famous for his outburst during the 1987 Florida State game, when, with the Hurricanes trailing 19-3, Irvin picked up a headset and began cussing out his coaches for not directing the offense his way (a precursor to Keyshawn Johnson's demands for the damn ball). Duly informed, the Miami coaches found a way to get Irvin the ball, and he found the way to score two touchdowns in leading the comeback charge that made the 'Canes' season.

He would display the same kind of emotion and athleticism in Dallas for seven seasons, over that time developing a style that exploited his size and power in getting to the ball, driving the city into a frenzied state of worship every time he crossed the goal line with one of Aikman's tosses and stretched out in his six-shooting celebratory routine.

Later, out on the town, all he had to do was drop the top of his 500SL — the one with the Playmaker vanity tags — then sit back and collect the phone numbers from the ladies. Dallas and all it had to offer was eager to embrace him. He had always admitted that he hungered for attention (he showed up for his grand jury testimony in a full-length mink coat). Irvin was not without his moments of doubt, however. "Just because I enjoy playing so much and don't mind dealing with the media and don't mind dealing with the cameras, everybody says I live for the glitz," he observed at the height of his success. "But all that glitters is not gold. The gold for me is playing the game. I try to have fun with it. You don't ever know when you'll cross this bridge again. So the best thing to do is take as many buckets as you can and fill them up with water and take them back with you."

He did that virtually every game, as his stats reflected (Irvin was usually good for at least 1,300 yards and better than a dozen touchdowns per season), with about the only negative being his sideline tirades. Most teammates wrote those outbursts off to Irvin's substantial competitiveness. "His mouth does roar," Smith, one of Irvin's best friends on the team, once explained. "But 'Maker always backs it up."

Indeed, he built a reputation for going hard every down, giving Aikman just the kind of crisp routes a quarterback needs in the chaotic face of a pass rush.

"Who can afford to loaf?" Irvin once asked. "The one time I loaf might be the one time that Troy needs me most."

The fifteenth of his family's 17 children, Irvin was raised in a three-bedroom house in Fort Lauderdale, Florida. The seven boys slept in one bedroom, the 10 girls in another. "I've been around a lot of people my whole life," he once explained. His father, Walter, was a roofer and lay minister, meaning that the family was poor in finances and rich in spirit. "There is no man who ever lived that I respect more than my father," Irvin has said. "He worked on the roofs sun up to sun down. He never complained."

When Irvin was 15, his father died of cancer and elicited a deathbed promise that Irvin would care for his mother, a chore that the star receiver has undertaken gladly, even expanding it to the range of the whole family. "I will never be a filthy rich man because I got to take care of too many people," he once explained. "It's a serious pleasure, not at all a burden."

In fact, little about his life seemed problematic right up to the point that it all came apart. He served his suspension over the '96 season, then returned to the floundering Cowboys, only to have the entire situation blow up in his face that December when Dallas police announced that he and Erik Williams were accused of sexually assaulting an exotic dancer. The woman later recanted her accusation (and Irvin would collect a handsome settlement from the media organizations that reported the news before it was confirmed).

Nevertheless, the damage had been done. Irvin realized just how bad it was during the ensuing offseason when his few public appearances were usually greeted by boos. He was startled at the fans' desertion of him, part of which figured into his talk of retirement. "I am not the most talented person in the world," he said at a press conference in June. "I played my game with intensity and emotion, and that made the difference…Right now, I just don't have that intensity…I don't have that love I used to have for the game."

His position irritated his teammates, particularly Aikman and Smith. Newton, however, took the comic route in his plea, telling Irvin through the media, "Mike, come on, man. Get your glare back, throw on some gold, and let's kick some ass."

The Playmaker must have heard him for he eventually returned to the fold. And Aikman even helped him back into corporate respectability, arranging in July for Irvin to sign a promotional deal with Logo Athletic. "I view the Logo Athletic deal as a sign that some people are telling me they believe in people. They're saying they believe things happen in life and things go wrong off the field but that some companies will still take a chance on you, and I truly appreciate it," Irvin said at the time. "When things get better, you look back and see that first company that stepped back with you, and you'll remember them just like I remember Nike for sticking with me."

Aikman, who plays a role in the company's decision-making, would not comment on the agreement.

"Troy Aikman means a lot to this company, and when he talks, we listen," Logo spokesman Eddie White told the *Dallas Morning News*. "Troy said he had a friend who was looking for something, and we decided to look into the situation.

"Michael Irvin is one of the greatest receivers in football, and between the white lines, he has been a great competitor," White added, saying perhaps more than he intended.

Those things, however, remain true about Irvin. He's still what he was: big, strong, fast and tough to defend. In other words, the Playmaker, a figure Texas finds hard to resist, particularly when so much of the Cowboys' prospects ride with him.

EMMITT

Like his good friend Irvin, Emmitt Smith also wants to make sure that he gets his fill. That much is evidenced by the rushing yardage Smith has stacked up.

"God put Emmitt Smith here to run with the football," Irvin once explained.

Since the Cowboys made him the 17th player taken in the 1990 draft, Smith has claimed four rushing titles, a passle of Pro Bowl appearances, and awards as both the league's regular season and Super Bowl Most Valuable Player.

Many consider him the Cowboys' most essential ingredient. "It's been proven," says Green Bay defensive end Reggie White. "They've won without Troy. They never win without Emmitt."

Former 49ers coach Bill Walsh says the 5-9, 209-pound Smith "is incomparable to any in the game today. He has a combination of speed, quickness, elusiveness, power and competitiveness that is unmatched."

Smith admits that his accomplishments and the accolades have him thinking about catching Walter Payton as the NFL's all-time leading rusher. Heading into the 1997 season, Smith had 10,160 career yards, ahead of Payton's totals at the same point in his career. But catching Payton will be far from easy, Smith acknowledged in 1994. "If anybody has a chance, it's me. When I won the first rushing title, people wondered if I was for real and if I could do it again. Then I won the second and they thought maybe I was for real. Then the third one made me legitimate. But now people want to know this: How long can Emmitt Smith be on top? I think I can be there a long time."

Smith's 1995 season was a giant reason the Cowboys claimed another Super Bowl title. He rushed for 1,773 yards (a 4.7 average) and 25 TDs. However, the 1996 campaign was one of frustration. His average yardage per game dipped below 4.0, and the season ended with observers questioning whether his best days were behind him, this despite the fact that he gained better than 1,200 yards last season and scored 12 touchdowns. Part of the problem was a pitiful Dallas passing game that meant every time Smith ran the ball he was greeted by an eight-man defensive front.

"We couldn't throw the ball last year when teams stopped our running game," Aikman admitted. "Unlike last year, I think we'll be able to throw the ball without any problems. Emmitt is healthy again and if teams decide to load up against him this time, they'll have to pay the price."

The once-sleek machine got an overhaul in the offseason — surgery to correct problems with bone spurs and chips. He, too, seemed eager heading into the '97 season, if not to claim redemption, at least to bash those who suggested he needed it.

Emmitt on da burn.

TROY BOY

Aikman has always had big aspirations. "I want to win a lot of Super Bowls," he says with that cock-eyed grin.

Of course the primary objective is to nail down number four now. His teammates figure if there's a quarterback to deliver on that promise, it's Aikman. "He's the best in the NFL, bar none," Irvin says.

Scheduled to turn 31 during the '97 season, the 6-4, 228-pounder remains the very definition of the modern pro. Cowboys scouting director Larry Lacewell once observed, "He possesses every ingredient you look for in a great quarterback. He's got nerves of steel. He's big, he's got a great quick release, he can scramble when he needs to. I really can't think of anything negative.

"If you were going to write up a program for 'the Guy,' he'd be it. Plus, I've got a Good-looking Guy theory. I think to be a great quarterback, you've got to be good-looking, and all of them are…He has the ingredients to go down as one of the all-time greats, if not the greatest."

Critics have long suggested that Aikman remains too interested in being tough, that he stays in the pocket far too long and subjects himself unnecessarily to the danger of the rush. His string of injuries has taught him to moderate that toughness. Now, he'll execute a hook slide on a scramble when he's about to be hit, or he'll ditch the ball prudently to avoid getting slammed.

But there's no question that he still challenges defenses, still seems intent on establishing that every game is his to control.

One of Aikman's secrets is his memory of his first two seasons in the league, when he missed 10 games due to injury. His first campaign, he guided the Cowboys to an 0-11 record, leading Johnson to brand him a loser. Eventually the quarterback and coach settled their differences, but not until after many angry, exasperating afternoons.

"I haven't forgotten that, and I don't want to," Aikman once explained. "I think having gone through that in '89, as painful as it was, has really helped me. Each year it makes me realize how fragile success is.

"It's very hard to win in this league. I was able to learn that my first year here. I've continued to remember that. With each game, with each season that goes by, it keeps me focused and keeps me continually wanting to go out and work and do the things necessary to give me a chance to be successful."

Unfortunately, the numbers sum up just about everything about his '96 season. Aikman threw 12 touchdowns against 13 interceptions. In the playoffs, the Cowboys got in scoring position three times against Carolina and had to settle for three field goals before finally getting a late TD. On the other hand, Aikman completed 63.7 percent of his passes, threw for better than 3,100 yards and finished with a decent 80.1 QB rating. He remains in the prime of his career, although he was said to have quietly threatened retirement if the Cowboys and

Troy Boy.

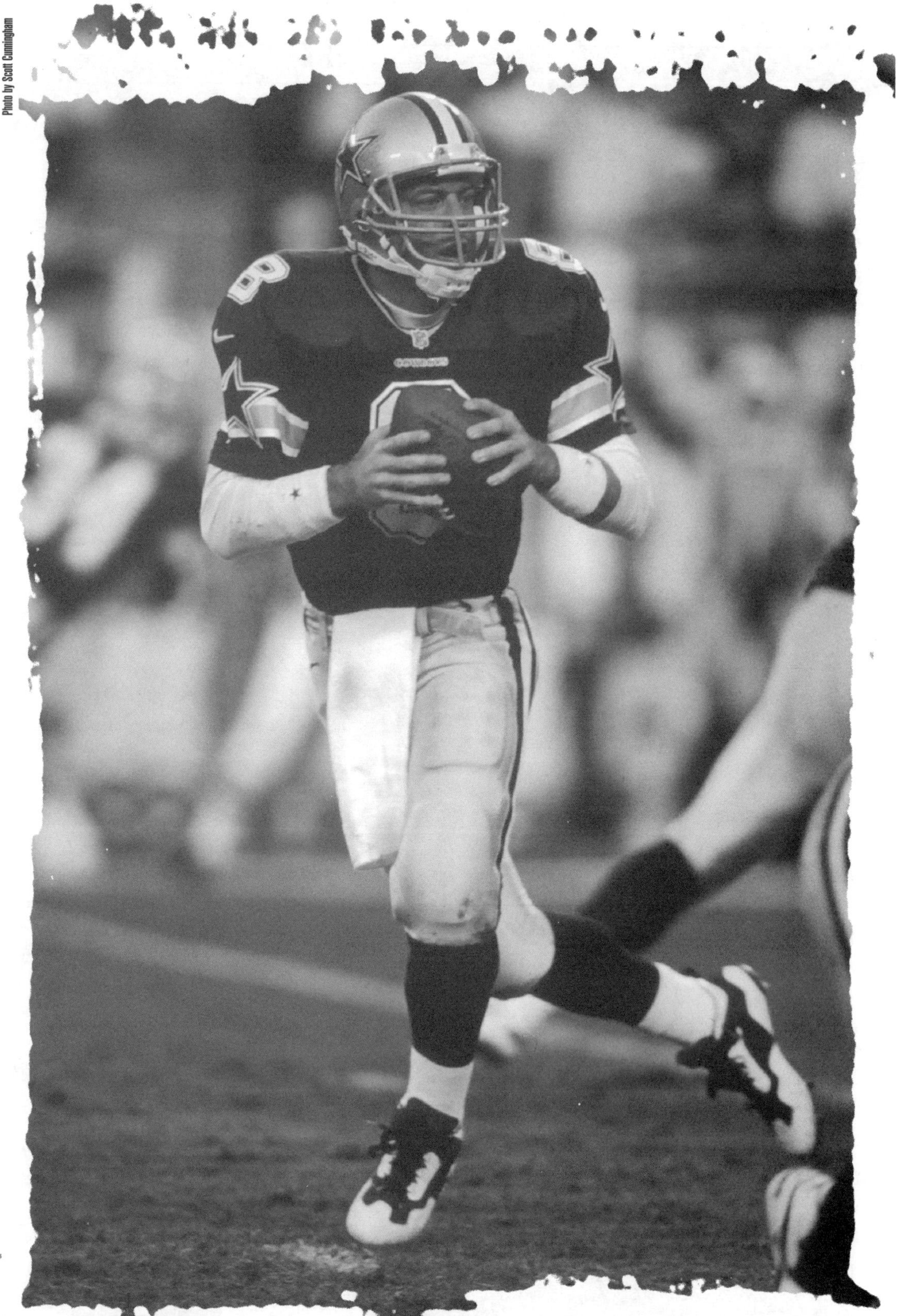

Photo by Scott Cunningham

Sundays are all business for Emmitt.

Chapter 12/Night Of The Living Cheeseheads

Photo by Vernon Biever

Holmgren has made it happen in the land of Cheeseheads.

've made the mistake of coming to Packerland, in part to search for the shiznit. I'm also here to try to understand the Cheesehead mentality that grows like a fungus on this franchise's legacy.

It's one of the first pretty spring days to hit the north country, and the Packers have wisely selected this weekend to open a mini-camp. Feeling some strange euphoria, there are several thousand fans clinging to the wire fences surrounding the outdoor practice field at the Don Hutson Center, the team's practice facility just across the street from its famed Lambeau Field. The Cheeseheads 'ooh!' and 'aah!' with every pass thrown in passing drills, never mind that the Packers are only in helmets and shorts. It's the first day of the new season, time to begin again. That's a paradox of sorts, because in Packerland, football season is never over.

"The excitement, hoopla around Packer football. . . it's unbelievable," marvels rookie Darren Sharper, a second round draft pick out of little William and Mary. "I wouldn't expect to have thousands of fans out watching practice. Only a few times in college did I get to play before big crowds. Here, you play before crowds in practice. It really makes you want to go out and work hard every day with that excitement."

Among the big Cheeseheads lining the practice field there are scores of little Cheeseheads, little girls with their hair braided out the back of their Packer hats, little boys with $59.95 miniature helmets and black markers, in anticipation of an autograph, all running the streets around the Packer complex here. Thousands of little Cheeseheads, accompanying big Cheeseheads. It's a mania, beyond any mania I've ever witnessed.

Johnny 'Blood' McNally, the son of a refined Wisconsin family, played for the Packers from 1928 to 1936 and helped them win four championships in those early roundhouse days. Writer Charles Pierce points out that McNally celebrated one victory by employing an entire brothel for his personal delight. "My parents tried to make me a cultured individual," Johnny Blood once explained. "But I had a very high resistance."

Somehow "high resistance" doesn't quite do these modern Cheeseheads justice.

Sure there are bunches of Chicago Bulls freaks dyed black and red just four hours south of here. But Bulls fans don't stalk the streets with the same zombielike fervor, the same weird-eyed stare like these Cheeseheads have. Whatever they got is dangerous. It makes you want to leave town before you drink too much of the water and get indoctrinated into the cult, the Krishna business that brings what might be an otherwise self-respecting adult to stand outside the team offices waiting for the Packer bus to empty after practice just to

Photo by Tim Umphrey

corner an autograph. And, no, it's not a business gig. They're not just looking for stars. They want the signatures of the offensive linemen and special teams guys, even the damn equipment guy, anybody with a hint of Packer connection.

This is a team that prides itself on community, and the practice field is just a short walk away from the locker room. The players and coaches used to make that walk after practice, but now the Packers have taken to coming to and from practice on a bus, just because they want to fend off the zombies. I don't blame 'em, either. The look in these people's eyes is frightening. It's Night of the Living Cheeseheads after dark around here.

As you might imagine, the whole air around this place is upbeat in the wake of their victory in Super Bowl XXXI. For example, the Packer Hall of Fame has port-o-potties. They're expanding and renovating the building, making room for the brilliant green horizons, the big gold future of Brett Favre and company.

An engaging part of this spectacle is Gordon "Red" Batty, the team's equipment man, who like most other minions in the league would go unnoticed if not for two things: 1) He manages the equipment of the Packers, and people notice everything about the Packers; 2) Broadcaster John Madden thinks so much of Batty's old-school enthusiasm that he named Red the most valuable player of the esteemed "All-Madden Team," the All-Star team the broadcaster selects every season.

An indication of Batty's class is that I have interviewed him for a couple of hours and not once has he mentioned his MVP status. Instead, his interest is focused on talking about the Pack's championship season.

"We got off to a very good start," Batty says, his eyes lit, "then we stumbled in Minnesota. But the guys bounced back, and they were very determined to do it. A lot of it, I feel, was based on the loss the year before in the championship in Dallas. Coming into the locker room after that game and realizing what they fell short of."

Indeed, the Packers had suffered a stinging defeat at the hands of the Cowboys in the 1995 NFC championship game. Green Bay had given up a lot of points early in the contest and stormed back at the end but couldn't overcome the Dallas lead.

Their efforts were chilled by the severe concussion sustained by assistant coach Gil Haskell, who was slammed to the ground when play crashed into him as he stood on the sideline. He had hit the deck with a sickly thud.

"To me that had a lot to do with the momentum in that game," Batty says of the injuries that required months of recovery for Haskell. "You can be driving down the highway and see a bad accident, and you're gonna slow down to 55 instead of running 70 all the time. It's a natural reaction."

The loss was painful for the Packers, but Batty sees it as the beginning of their rise to championship status the next year. "That's when the players came together," the equipment

Reggie is Green Bay's main minister.

manager says of the scene in the locker room after that loss in Dallas. "They had a special prayer together, then they spoke before the media had access to the locker room. They said some things that they were not going to let happen again."

Coach Mike Holmgren and his players talked about not losing focus, about keeping in mind what they had to accomplish, keeping in mind what was in store. Then, they went out in 1996 and virtually dominated the NFL to prove they had learned their lesson. Their return to the NFC championship game marked their coming full circle from the 1995 defeat.

"The most emotional moment," Batty said, "was beating the Panthers in the NFC championship game and the players all coming up the tunnel from the field into the locker room, knowing that they were going to the Super Bowl. There was a special gleam in everybody's eye, from Bob Harlan, the team president, down to the guys who play on the special teams and the people working on the staff. Everybody knew it was gonna happen."

Now the goal is to make it happen all over again.

"People are always throwing it up in our faces that we can't beat Dallas," says running back Edgar Bennett. "So you gotta always go out and prove yourself. Even if you win the Super Bowl one year, you gotta go out and do it again. Every year there's always something different. We don't want to be remembered as a team that just won it one year. We want to go out and add to it, as far as creating one of those type of dynasties that were here in Green Bay in the past. When people thought of Green Bay in the past, all they thought of was champions, of Titletown. We wouldn't mind bringing that back."

THE FREE AGENT

It is into this rare atmosphere that Eugene Chung, a former Virginia Tech All-America selection in 1991, has come to renovate his professional career, after stops in New England, Jacksonville and San Francisco.

The surprise might be that Chung, one of the few Asian Americans in pro football, would join the defending world champions when it would seem that he might have a better opportunity as a free agent with another organization. But that's not the way he sees it.

"What better organization to come to?" he says while munching a quick lunch in the locker room between practice sessions. "And there's so much history here, and there's also a history of players being happy here and being treated right. The decision isn't very hard when it comes to that. Some teams just have track records."

It says much that the Packers were eager to sign Chung, who had a three-year stint with New England after being selected by the Patriots with the 13th overall pick of the 1992 draft. In 1995, he was picked by the Jacksonville Jaguars in the expansion draft, stayed there one season, then moved to the 49ers for another frustrating year.

Both Bill Parcells, the coach who drafted him in New England, and Tom Coughlin, the big hoss in Jacksonville, are known as two of the NFL's most difficult people. After working with them, Chung went to San Francisco only to find a coaching staff on its way out.

"There were three guards for one spot, and I had a hard time adjusting to the finesse West Coast offense," he says. "I didn't have the greatest camp, and by the time I got it down, it was late."

Just before the '96 season, the 'Niners gave him his release. "You learn from things like that," he says. "And you do a lot of soul searching in the meantime. As a player, having time off, I finally realized why I play this game. The love of it, the camraderie. It's really not about the money. It's a job and not a bad one. Of course you're getting paid. But I did a lot of soul searching this past season. I had to think through why I played this game. I had plenty of time to think about it. It's probably one of the quietest, loneliest times a player could have."

No question it recharged his batteries, though. And just in time. Several teams came calling after his release, and he chose the Pack, even though they wanted him to change positions, from guard to center. Management figured him as an ideal upgrade for backup center, which means he has a solid chance of making the roster coming out of training camp.

It's a change he's excited about making.

"They expect the best; they want the best, and they'll settle for nothing less," he says of the Packers. That would seem to be the attitude around all organizations, but it isn't. "It makes you want to work harder, makes you want to be here.

"I've been here since March 16, training, getting the new offense down, just getting back into the swing of things," Chung says. "There was 16 inches of snow on the ground when I got into town. That was a big surprise. But after looking around the town and meeting some of the people, the people in this town are real friendly and nice, and that's different from where I just came from. In New England and San Francisco, that's real fast-paced. Here, it's a real nice pace.

"It's nice to be around this type of atmosphere with these kinds of players here," Chung adds. "They're receptive. And very welcoming. In San Francisco, you had to earn your way in and prove yourself. That makes it tough for some people. It was a little intimidating. It was interesting having so many marquee players there, though. You had Jerry Rice and Steve Young and all those defensive guys. There aren't many teams like that where you have so many household names. It was exciting, but along with it came a lot of intimidation. It was nuts, ya know."

It's obvious that now with his fourth team in six years Eugene Chung is well attuned to the paradoxes of pro sports. He supports the player movement brought by free agency all the while knowing that it has hurt his own career.

"Free agency has come a long way in football," he says. "It's here and probably will stay around for a long time. In the sense of fan support and unity, it's not so good. Fans want to see a lot of the same players back every year, and if they're changing teams every two years it's gonna be tough. But, still, in my experience, free agency has been good for the players. And I can't complain about that.

"If you really think about it, though, it does create a cynical atmosphere around the team. You'll have one guy tying up six or seven million in salary cap money. You have this high range and low range for players. You don't have the middle range people any more. It's a big drop. So that can be very cynical. You have a lot of resentment going around a team. Why are three people tying up $20 million of the cap and a lot of other people fighting for a minimum contract? When you think of it that way, it brings out the cynicism."

Coaches need to build team unity to be successful, but with the players on the team fighting over a pie of available money, unity can quickly get lost. That's why it takes special people to lead NFL teams, Chung says. "You look at teams like Dallas, which is a prime example. You have five or six guys at this high end, then you have the low end people. But that team unity is still there in Dallas. Teams like that, that can get across that salary structure bridge and still maintain unity, are the teams that win Super Bowls. Obviously, this team (the Packers) is like that, too.

"It's up to the coach to bring that together. And that's what coach Mike Holmgren does here, and Ron Wolf, the GM. They make everyone feel equal. Of course you have your superstars, but even that is subdued. There's no real egos on this team. You can walk around and look. There's no egos, no real attitudes here."

Red Batty can attest to that after the better part of three decades managing equipment for NFL and CFL teams. "The game has definitely changed. It's really a big business now," he says. "Attitude, money, the salary cap has made things more cynical. But last year in Green Bay, that was never a factor."

Having worked for the Houston Oilers, Batty knows how petty factors can disrupt a team. "All the great opportunities we had and let slip away in Houston," Batty says of teams brimming with talent but missing the essential ingredient. "I still shake my head over that. It was there. A couple of things didn't click. I can't really put my finger on it."

A little conflict here, a loss of focus there, an iota of selfishness at the wrong time, it doesn't take much to wreck a team's hopes. That's why Batty thrives on Green Bay's first championship season in 30 years.

"With Coach Holmgren's leadership and direction, it was just great to see that thing unfold," he says. "Each day in the locker room, each day in practice, each game on the road, at home. The way players would help each other out when one guy was down. How they would stay together. There were a couple of losses, like Kansas City, that just humbled them, and you need that."

So much of it was driven by players like All-Pro defensive end Reggie White, Batty says.

"The way he goes out there in Lambeau, and the way everybody just loves Reggie. As far as him dominating in a game, it's incredible."

Batty loves being on the sidelines during a game, where he can often sense when something is going to happen. He hears the defensive plays being called and sees formations developing.

"Sometimes," Batty says, "the extra defensive linemen will tap me on the shoulder and say, 'Watch Reggie on this play. Something's gonna happen.' Sure enough, it develops, and there's a great moment. It's just the way he plays, the way he dominates, the way he takes control of that defense on the field. The leadership. It's great to see it."

Of all the Packers, White's physical style epitomizes football's old-time smashmouth ethic. There's a sense of power that comes from being physically intimidating, plus the emotion of that power. "That's the way football is supposed to be played," Bennett says. "It's a physical rough game, a violent game. That's what football is all about. When we go out, we try to set the tone, so that when people think about Green Bay, they don't want to play us. That's the feeling we put into it."

Even in a minicamp that special attitude emanates from White, Chung says. "He's a presence. He's a force. And when he speaks, he's very articulate. He gets his message across."

As the 35-year-old White sees it, the age of free agency with constantly shifting team rosters makes veteran players all the more important. "Guys moving from team to team, that's a huge change," the defensive end says of the NFL today as compared to when he entered it 13 seasons ago. "Some younger guys, not all of them, really they've been successful in college, but now they've got to come in and learn how to win at this level. This game provides the opportunity to get a lot of money, but the thing is, that's not the ultimate goal. The ultimate goal is to win. So veteran leadership is important. Some people say this is a young man's game, but you need older guys to show the younger guys how to play.

"It's about the team," White says, a point the Packers will have to prove they understand this season. He knows that nothing can destroy a team like success. "It's a challenge to make sure we stay focused. Now all these teams are out to beat us. That means we've got to show some character."

"Our biggest challenge is staying together," Edgar Bennett agrees. "Doing what we did to be successful last year. We just got to stay together, keeping in mind that it's gonna take a team in order to get there. Don't put no one over the team."

He, too, knows that success has a way of pulling a team apart.

"This team is above that," he says, "and I think that's why we were able to win last year, because guys kept it within the team. Whatever we did was team oriented."

Holmgren is the primary guardian of that ethic. But so are White and Bennett and Eugene Robinson and Brett Favre. Perhaos the best leader of all the Packers is defensive back

Brett, Antonio and Robert Brooks run the show on O.

LeRoy Butler. "Butler's more of a vocal leader," Bennett says of the All Pro. "When he sees someone not getting it done, he'll speak up and say it. He's always been like that since I've known him. When it's time for somebody to say something to put a fire up under the members of this team, he's the perfect guy for it. He's made plays on the field; when he talks people are going to listen."

Except for all these Cheeseheads with the high resistance. The only thing they seem to hear are the whispers of Vince Lombardi's ghost. Then again maybe it doesn't matter. Because the legends in Green Bay, past and present, are all talking the language of winning.

Cheeseheads are fanatic about their Packers.

Epilogue

The onslaught of an NFL season always brings unexpected, often unwanted, developments. Take young Heath Shuler, for example. The last thing he needed was a passle of turnovers when he started his new quarterbacking job in New Orleans, but the interceptions and fumbles came in bunches, which in turn threatened the new start he had hoped to make under Coach Mike Ditka.

Although the Saints' offensive line struggled and Shuler was battered by opposing pass rushes, he somehow managed to avoid major injury over the season's first weeks. Others weren't so lucky. Packers running back Edgar Bennett tore an achilles tendon in the preseason and was lost for the year. Carolina quarterback Kerry Collins suffered a broken jaw in a preseason game and stirred controversy by using a racial epithet in addressing a teammate. Collins somehow shook off the injury and made it back into the lineup early in the season, only to be benched for a lackluster performance.

Jacksonville's Mark Brunell injured his knee in a preseason game and was projected to miss at least six weeks. However, he cited his faith in God and promised to return early, which he did, making his first start of the season before September was over.

San Francisco quarterback Steve Young, too, was rocked by a head injury, adding to his string of concussions, and bringing calls for his retirement to prevent brain damage.

Pittsburgh's Kordell Stewart also suffered a preseason knee injury but overcame it, only to struggle mightily in his team's season-opening loss to the Cowboys. Later, the Steelers would pull their record to .500, but the adjustment was painful.

The big news for folks in Dallas was the prime performance of Michael Irvin, who snagged seven passes for 153 yards and two TDs in the Cowboys' 37-7 demolition of the Steelers. The Playmaker's return lit up the Dallas offense and brought speculation that the Cowboys were headed for a collision with Green Bay. Strangely, the Cowboys continued winning although their offense was sluggish. September came and went without Emmitt scoring a rushing touchdown, which meant that the Cowboys struggled in the red zone.

The Packers, meanwhile, dropped the Bears to win their opener, although their performance was uneven and got worse from there. October dawned with the Packers trailing the surprising Tampa Bay Buccaneers in the Central Division and looking very vulnerable.

The Jets also had a big debut under Bill Parcells, drubbing the Seahawks in Seattle, 41-3. Wayne Chrebet caught two TD passes and Keyshawn Johnson added six receptions to his career totals. "We're working well together," said Jets QB Neil O'Donnell, who threw five TD passes. "Keyshawn's doing fine. He's doing what he's told to do. He's getting open. I have no problem with Keyshawn."

Indeed, the Jets, winners of just one game the season before, opened with a 3-2 record that included a near defeat of Bill Parcells' old team, the Patriots. In the process, Parcells took a genuine liking to Johnson, who in turn had taken on a new level of humility, even admitting that he had much to learn as a receiver, while emphasizing that he was very willing to learn.

"I like him," Parcells said of Johnson. "I enjoy being around him. I sincerely mean that. What I see is a hard-working kid."

One who quickly got a reputation as the best blocker among the Jets' wide receivers. "This kid is brave," Parcells observed. "He's not afraid. He'll hit. He'll take on linebackers, defensive ends. He's in good condition, has good stamina and doesn't seem to get tired in games."

"In order to get great, I've got to work," Johnson agreed.

Matching the intensity of Parcells' new team was that of his old club, the Patriots, who rolled over San Diego, 41-7, led by Drew Bledsoe's 340 yards and four touchdowns passing, and went on from there to a 4-0 start that made them look very much like a Super Bowl contender.

Across the league, there was joy and abject misery throughout the opening month, almost in equal quantities. There was also pain and blood, the products of a violent sport. But, as Green Bay's Edgar Bennett pointed out, that's the way it's supposed to be. After all, it's Smashmouth football.

Like we said at the top of the show, there have been literally hundreds of reprobates, mad dogs and lunatics drawn to the violence of Sunday mayhem over the decades. The sport began more than a century ago as a seedy business that grew out of the dreams and aspirations of a collection of rogue promoters, tramp athletes and sociopaths. Never did they fathom that today's players would become millionaires for their dirt-kickin', snot-slingin', eye-gougin', ball-bustin', bone-rattlin' antics. Which brings us again to this most essential question: Are the members of today's Attitude Generation able to live up to the indecency of their legacy, or has all the money made them little more than a bunch of wimp-ass show dogs, preenin' and prancin' for the cameras, who sneak away between plays to dial their stockbrokers on cell phones? Are they real football players, or just a bunch of high-priced phonies?

Let's put it this way. Their blood runs red and their teeth pop loose at odd angles when they get smashed in the face, just like in the old days. The pain is maybe even bigger, but so are the paychecks. Sure sounds like da shiznit to me.

Peace. If you can find it.